Alive
by
Grace

A Mothers Story with A Message of
Hope from Christopher

Suzanne Cavalier

and

Christopher Cavalier

*God Bless!
Chris Cavalier*

ISBN 978-1-64191-987-6 (paperback)
ISBN 978-1-64191-988-3 (digital)

Christian Faith Publishing, Inc.
832 Park Avenue
Meadville, PA 16335
www.christianfaithpublishing.com

Printed in the United States of America

Chapter 1

Introduction

My name is Suzanne Cavalier. I originally started putting these experiences on paper twenty years ago just to get them out of my head. The story was written from my perspective, with Christopher and his siblings as the intended audience. I wanted them all to understand what he had gone through and why our lives might have been different than others around us. However, while writing, I discovered that our experiences might offer hope and inspiration to others.

This story is for other families of children with catastrophic illness. You are not alone. Let Christopher's journey empower you with the knowledge and insight you will need to promote healing physically, emotionally, and spiritually, for you and your special child.

It is also for healthcare professionals, so that they might better understand the impact they can have on patients and their families, that a team approach is the best approach, and that healing may last a lifetime.

I was twenty-two years old and married to my husband Chris, or "Big Chris" as he would later be called, when I became pregnant with my first child. We were young, but excited and prepared to be parents. At least that is what we thought. Living in a small house in New Jersey, Chris was employed at a local electronics company and I was a dental assistant, though I wanted to be a full-time mother more than anything. My doctor gave me regular checkups and ultrasounds, and my husband and I attended childbirth classes together. We expected a typical birthing experience.

"Gravely ill." These were the words used to describe my first child shortly after his birth on August 21, 1986. I was at the hospital for only fifteen minutes when a nurse detected fetal distress. The doctor entered the room and immediately ordered a cesarean section. My only thought was, *Quick! Deliver my baby and everything will be fine.* The horrified look on my husband's face convinced me that this would not be the case. Moments later, our newborn son arrived. Before I could touch him, however, he was whisked off to the intensive care nursery.

Chapter 2

Horror and Hope

Ten years have passed, but I can remember the tragic birth of my first child like it was yesterday. It was a warm summer evening on Friday August 21, 1986. My labor started around three o'clock in the afternoon with mild contractions only three minutes apart. Having been to Lamaze class, I thought it would be several hours before I had to go to the hospital, so I began my wait. At about five o'clock, I called my husband Chris at work. He calmly encouraged me to relax and told me he would come home when he had finished his last job. Within minutes of our conversation, my water broke. I called my doctor, and he told me to come directly to the hospital to be checked out. I called Big Chris at work again, and he dropped what he was doing to take me to Mercer Medical Center in Trenton, NJ. We arrived at six-thirty that evening, full of the excitement and anticipation that most new parents have. The nurses quickly hooked me up to a monitor, while my husband went downstairs to the business office to check me in. Within moments, the nurse detected a problem. She called for assistance to check the baby's condition. The attending physician placed an internal monitor on the baby's head in an unsuccessful attempt to hear a heartbeat. A second frantic attempt was made to find the baby's heartbeat, but it was not there.

Doctors and nurses began rushing all around me while I lay there shocked and confused. I focused on the moment that I would see my baby, when this would all be over and we would celebrate this new life inside me.

My obstetrician arrived and immediately ordered a cesarean section. He told me to stay still and cooperate, and that it would all be over in a few minutes. Honestly, my first reaction was, "Great!" The moment I had waited nine months for had finally arrived. I had no idea how serious the problem was. They whisked me off to the operating room with a nurse starting an IV as we were going down the hall. The frightened look on my husband's face made it clear to me that something was horribly wrong. My body began to tremble with fear as we neared the operating room. Big Chris was not allowed in, but had to stay out in the hall as we went through the doors. The contractions were intense. I remember my doctor telling me that there was no time to prep for surgery. The OR nurse poured a cold bucket of Betadine solution over my exposed belly, while the anesthesiologist assured me I would be okay.

Three minutes later, our son was born. He was blue and unable to breathe on his own, but alive. His enlarged chest and sunken abdomen led the doctors to believe he had serious complications. Something was terribly wrong, but no one knew just what. They took the baby straight to the special care nursery, hoping to stabilize him and diagnose the problem. The neonatologist took over along with the special care nurses, pediatricians, and respiratory technicians. They took an X-ray of the baby's chest and abdomen and quickly gave us a diagnosis.

Our baby was born with a congenital diaphragmatic hernia (CDH). He had a hole in his diaphragm that allowed his intestines to migrate up into his chest cavity, compressing his lungs. They could not inflate, so he could not breathe. This is a rare and unusual birth defect found in only one out of 12,500 live births, and never seen before at Mercer Hospital.

The outlook for our baby was quite grim, but the people at Mercer were incredible, as they began life-saving efforts to keep our newborn son alive. They placed our tiny baby on life support, attaching his little body to a profusion of tubes, wires, and monitors.

I was sleepy from the general anesthesia when my obstetrician came to me and told me that I had a very sick little boy. I heard him mention the word "hernia" and I focused my thoughts on that. It was a familiar word to me, and I knew surgery could correct hernias. I felt confused by all of the concern and sadness I detected in the people around me. Slowly the anesthesia wore off, and it became clear to me that I might lose my baby. When Big Chris finally came to see me, it was obvious that he had been crying. He just kept repeating, "It's bad, hon, really bad, and I don't know what to do." He held me in his arms and we cried together, feeling helpless and scared, not for the last time. My husband tried hard to be strong. He wanted to tell me everything would be all right, but his distress showed through, and that worried me. I asked him to go to be with our son and make sure that they never gave up. I told him that our baby would survive and we had to be strong for him. God could not take my baby away. I had not even seen him yet.

Big Chris went back to the special care nursery with his parents, while my parents stayed with me in the recovery room. In the meantime, a surgeon had been called in from Robert Wood Johnson University Hospital about an hour away. The surgeon, Dr. Jeffrey Zitsman, arrived later that Friday evening to repair the baby's diaphragm. I took it as a sign of hope that the doctor would even operate. Dr. Zitsman examined our baby and then met with us. He explained that our son was a very sick little boy, and that he might not survive the extensive surgery. He held my hand as he told us that he would do his best, but in all honesty, it did not look good. We had no choice but to give our consent to the surgery and pray that our son would survive. A Catholic priest came in and baptized our baby before he went to the operating room.

For three agonizing hours, the entire family waited as we cried, fearing for the baby's life. Would we ever be able to hold him or even touch him? What about the dreams we had for him? Should we hang on to the hope that a newborn baby is strong enough to survive this surgery? Can he beat the odds that are already against him? It all felt unreal, like a nightmare. Our lives had changed in an instant, never to be the same again. I kept telling myself that if I remained strong, my baby would live. Apprehensive about God's will for my newborn son, I selfishly wanted him kept alive no matter what it would take.

I couldn't bear to lose him. We told the doctors to do everything humanly possible to save our baby boy. They did.

*****

Doctor Zitsman came out of the operating room and right to my side. He had lowered the baby's intestines from the chest cavity back into his abdomen and sewed a synthetic patch in place to repair the defect. Dr. Zitsman explained that the baby had survived the surgery, but cautioned that his lungs were unusually tiny. They never had the chance to grow and mature due to the obstruction of the intestines. The doctor gave our firstborn son a two percent chance to live. He did not expect our baby to survive the night.

I felt paralyzed with the fear of losing my baby. It was the longest and most terrifying night of my life. My strong and courageous husband cried in a chair beside my bed, while our families kept watch over their new grandson. The woman beside me and her healthy baby girl were moved to another room, while the hospital staff worked diligently together, caring for Big Chris and me, as well as our baby. Although everyone was somber, I had a strange sense of hope deep down in my heart that my baby was going to live. God couldn't take him away from me, not before I could see him or touch him.

At six o'clock in the morning, a nurse came in and encouraged me to go to the nursery, but something inside kept me back. I felt that if I stayed away, my baby would have to live longer, until they could figure out what to do next to prolong his life. I guess it was just my way of coping. Besides, everyone said he was a beautiful, healthy-looking child, and for now, that was enough to satisfy me.

Later that morning, the neonatologist came in with a more positive look on his face. He and Dr. Zitsman explained that a relatively new procedure known as Extra-Corporeal Membrane Oxygenation or "ECMO" might be our son's only chance for survival. A rush of excitement came over me, and I remember crying out with delight. No matter how grave the situation, there was still a ray of hope. He continued to explain that it could be a very long process, and that life support by ECMO was still in its experimental phase. There were only seven machines in the United States, and strict criteria were applied for transport and acceptance.

This was incredible news, and through the prayer chains that had already been set up, people all over New Jersey began praying for our son. He was already a miracle, touching the lives of many caring and concerned people. Everyone was pulling together for one tiny baby that I had not even laid eyes on yet. Hours passed as they searched for an ECMO center for my baby. At three o'clock in the afternoon, the neonatologist told us that Boston Children's Hospital had accepted him as a candidate for ECMO. They would send a jet and a transport team to New Jersey to pick up our son. Cheers seemed to fill the maternity ward as everyone celebrated the good news with us. I knew in my heart the doctors were doing everything they could to save his life, though I found out later that Boston Children's had never successfully treated a CDH infant using ECMO.

A transport team arrived late that evening. They were an amazing group of people and confident about the transport to Boston. It all seemed so unbelievable. My newborn baby was going on a jet to a strange city for an experimental procedure, with a small chance of success, and we had consented. There was no time to waste; every minute was critical to his survival.

The transport doctors first sat down beside me and asked what the baby's name was. Everyone on the floor had referred to him as the "sick" baby. The physician said, "Well, I need to know what to call him!" I hesitated for a moment because no one had asked us that before. Giving him a name would make it all so real, but we already had one picked. "Christopher," I said. "After his father." The doctor then offered to escort me down to see my baby before they left. She assured me that my son was beautiful, healthy, and normal-looking. These were the words I needed to hear. However, she also warned us that there was a definite possibility our baby would not survive the flight, and that they would maintain contact with us.

I was numb from my head to my toes, but with Chris's encouragement, I forced myself to go to my baby and face reality. I went down the long hall to the special care nursery, so full of emotion and anticipation. What would he really look like? Why did this happen to us? Are we making the right decision? What did I do wrong? I felt as if everyone was watching me for my reaction, and I was determined to remain strong and hopeful.

Peering in at my baby, my world slowed for a moment as I saw the face of an angel. I was able to see right past the tubes and wires to the most precious baby I had ever laid eyes on. Then reaching out, I touched him on the top of his tiny head. His skin felt soft and warm. I held him close to my heart and said a prayer to God, asking him to watch over my son. I never truly said goodbye because I felt in some way that a part of me was going with him to Boston.

Chapter 3

The ECMO Team

Saturday evening at eleven o'clock, my baby was on his way to Boston Children's Hospital, while I remained in a hospital bed in New Jersey. ECMO was his only chance for survival, and I was truly grateful for the two percent chance that my baby boy will survive. As the hours passed, it became difficult to remain optimistic. There were no flowers or balloons, and no congratulations. It was all different from what I had anticipated. I did not know whether to prepare myself for the worst or hope for the best. I did learn rather quickly, however, to focus on the moment and not look ahead. Several grueling hours passed before we finally got a call that the plane had landed at Logan airport and they were on their way to Boston Children's. At four o'clock in the morning, we received a call that transformed our worries into tears of joy. My baby had been successfully placed on ECMO.

Christopher had been given another chance at life. It was truly something to celebrate, and I knew he had gone to a great place. Everyone cautioned me about my optimism, but I trusted that the heroic effort of so many people was for a reason. It just had to work. The next morning, Big Chris and my brother Paul prepared to fly to Boston to see Christopher, while I was to stay in the hospital long enough to recover from the C-section. One exceptionally understanding nurse encouraged me to bottle my breast milk for Big Chris to take to my baby. To think I could help in some way was a wonderful idea. They packed the tiny bottles of breast milk in a small Igloo cooler, which went off with Big Chris to the airport. A team of

ECMO specialists greeted Big Chris and Paul when they arrived and took them to the baby. Big Chris was shocked and overwhelmed by the machinery and equipment, but felt comforted by the dedication and professionalism of the people who were caring for Christopher. They encouraged Big Chris to touch his baby and take pictures of him to bring home. Then they explained the ECMO machine to him and familiarized him with the workings of the hospital's multi-disciplinary intensive care unit.

Big Chris and Paul returned to New Jersey later that same evening and came directly to my hospital. Big Chris actually came into the room, laughing and smiling as he described his experience in Boston. He bragged about how wonderful the people were and assured me that my baby was in perfect hands—that everything humanly possible was being done for him. Big Chris brought photos of Christopher hooked up to a room full of machinery. They were very difficult to look at; Christopher's body appeared swollen, and he was unclothed and covered with numerous tubes and wires. He had looked so normal and healthy to me before he left. I could only hope we had made the right decision. Big Chris also brought home names and phone numbers, so I could call the Boston staff myself with any questions or concerns.

The folks at Mercer Hospital continued to be supportive and concerned for our well-being throughout our ordeal. They understood and even shared in our pain, which meant a great deal to me. I needed that sense of team solidarity. Many of the nurses spoke of personal experiences of loss and tragedy, and it helped to know I was not alone. Sensing that my family members wanted to make my pain go away, I often found myself trying to be strong for them. I also continued pumping and saving my breastmilk to take with me when I was released. It gave me a sense of hope that, somehow, I could be a part of our baby's healing and survival.

*****

Two days later, I left the hospital. I had no baby in my arms, but a very precious one in my heart. I had a deep yearning to see him again. Big Chris and I went home and began packing for the drive to Boston. I did not want to waste any time, nor did I want to be in the house long enough for my emotions to get the better of me. It was a relief to find that all the baby items had been put away in the baby's room with the door shut. I held on to the hope that we would bring him home one day, and the nursery would be complete.

It felt so strange to travel six hours to a faraway city to see my newborn son. So much happened to me in the past five days, and now I was about to see my baby on ECMO. The doctors had explained the machine over the phone, and I had seen pictures, so I thought I was prepared.

We arrived at Boston Children's Hospital on a sunny summer day, simultaneously full of excitement and fear. My husband must have forgotten that I had just gone through major surgery, because he sprinted up the stairs and almost ran down the hall to the elevators. After catching up to him, we entered the intensive care waiting room to be greeted by Dr. Pearl O'Rourke. She was the physician in charge that day and was going to take me to my baby. She ushered us through two large doors that opened into a huge room full of people and high-tech machinery. I started walking slowly towards this ECMO conglomeration, not realizing my baby was at the center of it all. On a tiny bed lay his naked body, pink and motionless. Alive, but not breathing. Peaceful, but not sleeping.

ECMO is a life-support procedure, similar to a cardiac bypass that allowed Christopher's lungs to rest and develop. Catheters were surgically inserted into his jugular vein and carotid artery. Blood was removed through the jugular vein, circulated through an oxygenator, rewarmed, and returned to the baby through his carotid artery. The machine effectively acted as an artificial set of external lungs. In order to inflate his lungs, the baby was sedated and put on a ventilator, which required a tube that entered through his nose and travelled down his trachea to his lungs. A tube for intravenous feeding and a multitude of various monitoring wires were also necessary.

My eyes welled with tears and my legs grew weak as both Big Chris and Dr. O'Rourke put their arms around me, and stood with me in silence. They knew I needed a moment to take it all in before

I could even utter one word. As I looked around, I realized this was truly an amazing place. The compassion of the attending staff for my child helped me feel at ease. The doctors explained everything to us in as much detail as we needed. We understood the workings of the ECMO machine and the purpose of each tube and wire attached to our baby. They even answered the questions we didn't know how to ask. Their sensitivity was comforting, and their sincere concern for our involvement meant the world to me. We had become part of the team, and at least for now, I no longer felt alone.

Chapter 4

Smooth Sailing

We were told Christopher could be expected to be on ECMO for at least five to seven days. During that time, chest X-rays and oxygen levels would be used to monitor his progress and determine the degree of lung growth and healing. After six days of treatment, the doctors decided to give Christopher a trial run off of ECMO. We were thrilled about the progress Christopher had made and were really starting to feel confident about his chances.

The lines from the ECMO circuit were clamped, and the baby was supported by mechanical ventilation only. Big Chris and I eagerly left the bedside to talk in greater detail with the surgeon who was responsible for our son. It was a moment I will never forget as long as I live. The surgeon's name was Dr. Craig Lillehei. In a steady voice, he explained the horrifying details of our baby's prognosis. By no means was our baby out of the woods. He told us it was a good sign that Christopher could be taken off ECMO, but that the road ahead was likely to be lengthy and uncertain. His condition was still critical and might remain that way indefinitely. Dr. Lillehei reminded us of the experimental nature of the procedure and the severity of Christopher's hernia. Though he assured us he would do everything he could to save him, he was unable to share much hope or long-term information. After all, babies like Christopher usually did not survive.

Dr. Lillehei made it clear that the greatest risk and danger of ECMO was hemorrhaging in the brain. He explained that a blood thinner, heparin, was being used to keep Christopher's blood flowing through the tubes. This significantly increased the risk of bleeding in the brain, which could cause brain damage. He assured us, however, that an ultrasound was performed daily to detect any major bleeds, and that Christopher seemed to be fine at this time. He did not discuss long-term neurological damage in our son, but I knew it was a possibility. I felt frozen with fear and virtually unable to speak or cry. Dr. Lillehei sat with us for a long time as we slowly began to ask some questions. I was desperate for a positive word concerning the prospect of my son's survival. A two percent chance was all he could give us.

I believed Dr. Lillehei needed my support to continue, and I wanted him to know that I could deal with whatever lay ahead as long as he never gave up. I could sense his compassion for my son and felt he truly understood our pain and anguish. From that moment with Dr. Lillehei, I never doubted that my child would receive the best care. I was strangely proud to be the mother of such a special miracle baby.

Christopher underwent surgery again that evening to remove the catheters from his neck. He had been on ECMO for nearly seven days at this point. The carotid artery and jugular vein used for ECMO were permanently closed. The risk of blood clots forming in these vessels and traveling to the brain was too great, so the blood flow was never re-established.

We left the hospital after his surgery that evening full of mixed emotions. Our newborn son lay back there like "property" of the hospital. His life dangled by a thread, and ours was on the edge of a rocky cliff. We felt helpless and out of control. How could you possibly have hope when everyone who came in contact with this baby said he was probably going to die? But again, how could you not have hope when these same people were taking such heroic measures to save his life? How could something happen to him now that he had come so far? These questions seemed to consume both of us as we walked next door to our hotel room in a silent embrace. It took all of my energy not to cry, for fear I would not be able to stop. I felt as if I had to be strong and optimistic for Big Chris. After all, he had to deal with work and finances back in New Jersey, and he didn't need a hysterical wife on top of it. It all seemed crazy, almost like a dream. Here we were, in a strange city three hundred miles away from our home, family, and friends. None of it seemed real or even possible.

When we got to our hotel room, Big Chris asked, "Why are we here? Did we make the right decision? Will our lives ever be the same again? If our son lives, will he be a normal kid and come home to live with us in New Jersey?" Of course, I had no answers, and I began to sob hysterically. The two of us cried together for a long time, unable to comfort each other. We sat awake for one of the longest nights of our lives, waiting for the phone to ring, signifying that something horrible had happened to our son. The dreaded call never came.

Finally, the sun came up. Thank God for mornings! Christopher had made it through his first night off of ECMO. We quickly showered, dressed, and hurried over to the hospital. As we entered the lobby, the smell of antiseptic turned my stomach. The elevator ride to the ICU seemed to last an eternity. We entered once again through the large double doors, where the receptionist greeted us with a smile. I thought that was a good sign, and when the attending physician came out, she was smiling too. She seemed excited about the baby's progress through the night, and sounded quite positive about a future for Christopher. It was a little confusing, but I think she must have had a reason for her optimism. We soon realized that each nurse and doctor had his or her own personality and bedside manner.

As I went into Christopher's room, I noticed a small note taped to the top of his bed:

MY NAME IS CHRISTOPHER.
Please call my mom every day at 11:00 AM.

The note also had red, white, and blue sail boats along the bottom, symbolizing the name the primary nurse had given Christopher. She named him the "Smooth Sailor" because he was their first baby to have survived off ECMO. The note had obviously been made with love. We sat with our baby for hours while talking to the nurses and respiratory technicians about our son and all the equipment. Big Chris took great interest in the ventilator settings and learned as much as he could about the machines. He focused on the settings and the numbers, and how they affected our son. This was his way of coping with the stress. I asked more about the baby's comfort, the medications, and the personal insights and opinions of the nurses, who seemed experienced and knowledgeable. Their insights led us to believe that the chances for our baby's recovery were still uncertain. His condition changed by the hour. Everyone agreed that his recovery would take several weeks on the ventilator and maybe months in the hospital, but they had at least started talking about our son's survival.

For the next few weeks, my husband and I traveled back and forth to Boston together. I could not bear it emotionally to stay in Boston without Chris by my side. I told myself that God could not take my baby away from me while I was not there. While I was home, I kept a journal of Christopher's slow and steady progress. Each morning, the nurse in charge would call with a detailed description of Christopher's condition and their plan for the day. They also gave us a toll-free number to call in the evening to get a report of the day's events. The nurses were absolutely wonderful, and Christopher had one assigned to him and only him at all times. We knew he was always receiving the best care and attention, and that kept me sane.

Each Friday, we would return to Boston either by plane or car. It never got any easier entering the hospital, and leaving got a lot more difficult. The doctors remained cautious about being too optimistic regarding the long-term prognosis, especially while Christopher was still on the ventilator. But the attitude of the nurses and technicians at his bedside was just the opposite. They took great pride in his successes and encouraged us to bond with our baby by changing his diaper and bathing him, even while he was still intubated. We were able to hold him and take lots of pictures to share with our family back home. They also told us to bring in a music box or soft music to play. My favorite thing to do was to rub Johnson's baby lotion on his tiny dried out feet because the smell would cling to my hands for the rest of the day. I found myself using it at home just to smell that wonderful baby smell and forget the distance between us.

His nurses, especially Margie Smith and Margie Rosenthal, were very special to us. They capably kept us informed and always exuded compassion. It was obvious that the doctors had a great respect for these nurses as they had for each other. When it was time to leave on Sunday evenings, we were always comforted by the thought of the special attention and quality of care our baby received from each and every one of them. What a blessing they were to us!

*****

September 11, 1986, at eight o'clock in the morning, we received a call from Christopher's primary nurse, announcing that our son was removed from the ventilator. His lungs had grown enough for him to breathe on his own, and he only needed the aid of an oxygen hood. It was a miracle he had come so far in only three weeks.

Big Chris and I arrived that Friday evening to find our baby lying on his belly, looking for the first time like a regular baby. There were no breathing tubes, chest tubes, IVs, or wires coming out of his body. He seemed normal, beautiful, and healthy, but there was something else about his appearance that struck me. He was wearing clothing. It was a one-of-a-kind outfit, handmade by Elaine Caron, his primary nurse. Elaine had celebrated his progress by sewing him a special blue "smooth sailor" outfit with sailboats across the front of it. I could only think what an amazing person she must be. We had not even met her yet (because she only worked the night shift), but she was already a significant person in our lives.

Our baby and the miracle of his survival had touched her heart. It was a great comfort to know that someone so caring and wonderful was with him through the night. Once again, I must have used avoidance tactics to cope with the situation because I did not feel like I needed to meet her yet. I had a great relationship with Christopher's daytime caregivers, and I feared breaking the bond Elaine had with my child. It might sound silly, but at the time, I would not have done anything that might interfere with the quality of care that my baby received. Subconsciously, I thought of her as his "Boston Mom." I was thrilled at the idea that she was so close to Christopher, so why step in and ruin a good thing?

I could not have asked for a better team of nurses. All of them had a way of comforting us even at the worst of times and celebrated with us at the best of times. I have great respect for the dedication and commitment they showed my son. On that wonderful day, as we celebrated his smooth sailing off the ventilator, I asked everyone their personal opinion of his quick progress. I always preferred getting multiple opinions, since I could simply pick the one that sounded best. One respiratory therapist said, "A year from now, it will all be just a bad memory." Oh, how I wish that were true.

Family and friends back home always asked us, "How can you be happy and smiling when your baby is so sick and far away?" Our reply was simple, "He is alive and doing well today! And he is being treated like royalty." Sure, it was extremely difficult, but it was almost as if our lives were in a time capsule and the rest of the world kept going. We lived day-by-day, hour-by-hour, and sometimes minute-by-minute. We focused all our energies on Christopher's survival and his well-being. The bottom line was that we did not have a choice. The only alternative was death.

*****

One week later, our smooth sailor was ready to be moved out of the intensive care unit down to the surgical floor. I was petrified. "How can this be?" I wondered. They had told us he might be in the ICU for months. "Are they sure he is really ready? Couldn't they keep him upstairs for a few more days until I was sure?" Big Chris and I had been conditioned into thinking the worst. For four long weeks, we were faced with a grim outlook for survival, and now Christopher was progressing out of intensive care. We should have been happy, but it was a frightening and insecure feeling. Christopher was going to a "regular" floor, but he was not a "regular" baby. There would not be a nurse at his side twenty-four hours a day, and we would have to get to know a whole new set of people. Would they realize how special he is?

Christopher actually made the transition just fine, but it took me some time to be comfortable and confident again. Soon, the nurses began feeding Christopher by mouth. It was pretty exciting to see him with a bottle. My breastmilk was still being used with calorie supplement, and whatever he did not drink by mouth was put through a nasogastric tube directly to his stomach. Though several attempts were made to feed him by mouth, Dr. Lillehei felt that a gastrostomy tube would be necessary to provide sufficient nutrition when he came home. I think that was the first time he mentioned Christopher going home. We never questioned the feeding tube and always trusted in our doctors' decisions. Besides, Christopher had such a difficult time eating and breathing at the same time. Certainly, breathing was the high priority. Surgery was performed, and a "G" tube was placed directly into his stomach. We were told to get ready because he could come home ten days later.

We were in shock! I quickly learned to take the good with the bad. How can I be upset with the tube feedings when I can take my miracle baby home? It seemed so routine there. If I was alone, I may have broken down hysterically, torn between hope and fear. (I think every children's hospital should have a room where parents could go and just scream.) However, I did not show my distress. I thought I should be strong and hide my fears. If I broke down, they might think I could not handle my own baby and that the struggle was too much for all of us, so I remained strong, in fear that God would take away my son.

Christopher's overall condition was quite stable at this point. He required oxygen by nasal cannula and physical therapy to keep his lungs clear. He was treated for reflux, fed primarily via gastric tube, and his fluids were regulated by diuretics and potassium supplements. Nevertheless, Christopher was finally becoming a normal baby. Making eye contact and smiling, his wonderful personality began to shine through. We felt ready and eager to bring him home. We wanted to share this special baby with the entire family.

I decided to stay with Christopher that final week and learn all I could about his care and schedule. The nurses were exceptionally kind and understanding. They taught and encouraged me to do everything for him, enabling me to bathe him, change his g-tube dressing, and start his feedings. I got up during the night with him, and greatly enjoyed any chances to be with him and care for him. He was quite a project. Of course, with the nurses' help and guidance, it did not seem so bad. I dressed him up every day in one of the many outfits we had received as gifts. Then I would just hold Christopher and rock him all day long. There was a lot of lost time I had to make up for, and I could hardly take my eyes off him. He was such a happy baby for all he had been through. His big brown eyes seemed to sparkle, and he smiled at anyone who entered the room. I was remarkably grateful for his nurses who allowed me to finally provide care and emotional support for my own child, and the opportunity to bond with him.

Christopher was in a small room with five other babies. At night, I would sign up for a cot and find a spot to try and get some sleep. That was nearly impossible. So many babies would be crying, and I would lie there, thinking about all the nights he was alone without his mom. At six o'clock in the morning, I would scurry to the shower and quickly get ready for the day. At seven, the residents would make their rounds, and I made it a point to hear what they had to discuss for the day. It was another good way of getting an impression of my son's progress. If they had positive things to say, I was set for the day; if not, I knew I could ask Dr. Lillehei when he came around later. By the end of the week, I was more than ready to bring Christopher home. I even learned how to do suction and CPR. They were both required before discharge. Our primary nurse began the paperwork, as I began all the arrangements for home. The social worker made the preparations for oxygen to be delivered as well as feeding supplies and visiting nurses. (Our insurance would not give us any nursing coverage at this time.)

Big Chris came with my parents to pick me up in Boston. They borrowed a large custom van from a friend to be sure we had enough room for all of Christopher's supplies and belongings. It was the most exciting moment to share with my husband. They arrived at eleven o'clock that evening very excited as well. We all went to a hotel to be sure of a good night sleep, and when we arrived back at the hospital early the next morning, Christopher was sleeping soundly. Hours passed and he was not waking as usual. Everyone joked that he was getting ready for the long ride home, but something inside me said this was not normal.

Chapter 5

A Mother's Intuition

A mother's intuition should never be questioned. By mid-afternoon, I had waited long enough, and I tried to wake Christopher. He was usually such a light sleeper, but he would not respond to me at all. Though his color was fine and his breathing seemed normal, I panicked and called for a nurse. At first, everyone thought I overreacted, but I persisted that something was wrong with my baby. The nurse tried everything to wake him, but he was limp and lifeless. I begged them to bring him back to the ICU, knowing they would understand what to do for him. The surgical staff remained calmed, but I demanded they call a physician immediately. Within minutes, Christopher was brought to the treatment room down the hall. We were asked to wait outside until they could determine the problem. This seemed odd to me, since we were usually welcomed to stay with our child.

They began testing Christopher for all sorts of things. Blood gas tests, chest X-rays, and a lumbar puncture were done right away, and we were informed that he never opened his eyes during these procedures. The doctors were obviously puzzled as to what was wrong.

Maybe this was it. Maybe he was never meant to go home, and his fragile body could not take it anymore. Standing outside frozen with fear once again, I put my ear to the door, just waiting to hear his weak cry, unable to even look at my husband or my parents. The sadness and disappointment were overwhelming. I could not bear to have my child suffer any more than he had already. The pain in my heart was as intense as any mother would feel in this situation.

We had no answers for several hours, and Dr. Lillehei could not be reached. I knew I would feel much more at ease if he was there. Christopher was eventually transferred back to the ICU for observation, yet everyone seemed to be calm and confident that he would be okay. I could not help but feel sorry for the staff who were all so proud of his amazing progress.

Desperate for answers, I stayed with my baby as long as I could. Big Chris and my parents insisted that we go back to the hotel for some sleep. Despite my own wishes, I left with them to the hotel that was twenty miles away. At about four in the morning, the telephone rang. Having been warned in the past that a doctor would only call with bad news in the middle of the night, I agonized over answering the call. I slowly picked up the receiver as I prayed for strength to handle the news. The attending physician explained in a soft voice how Christopher's condition had worsened—that he was intubated and put back on the ventilator. It seemed he spiked a temperature and had an infection somewhere. He also retained high levels of carbon dioxide, which explained why he was so unresponsive.

I could not imagine how to react to this horrible news. Part of me was relieved to know he was still alive, but another part was so angry that this happened to him. I was encouraged to wait until morning to come back to the hospital. Doctor Lillehei had been contacted, and I felt more at ease knowing that he was aware of the incident.

We arrived back at Boston Children's early the next morning with the same fear as the very first day. As I saw his tiny unclothed body back on life support, my heart simply crumbled. His eyelids were slightly opened, so I asked his nurse to please close them for me. I knew he was heavily sedated, but I could not bear to look into those empty blue eyes, and I did not want him to see me in such distress. His nurse that morning was Pat Berry. She knew all of us and shared in our sadness. She stood by me not saying a word, knowing that nothing she could say would make a difference at that moment. I had utmost respect for her insight in allowing us the time to express our deep emotions. Sometimes, the best thing to say is nothing. I looked down at my baby, and as I wound the wheel of his musical ducky, tears began streaming down my face. I truly did not know how to handle the situation, but I knew I needed to do it in my own way at my own pace, and for my own good. For the first time, it did not matter what anybody else thought of my grief.

Several minutes later, Dr. Lillehei arrived. He entered the bed area with a look of confidence. He reassured me that Christopher received the appropriate care throughout the night, and reminded me how strong my baby was compared to the day he arrived. He explained that this was a setback to be expected with such a vulnerable baby, describing the ventilator as a friend rather than an enemy. His plan was to get him over whatever infection this was and to have him breathing on his own again in a few days. I put all my faith and trust in him as I had done in the past. It was obvious by now that he would not give us any false hope. Just as predicted, Christopher was extubated two days later and sent back to the surgical floor with expectations of going home a week later. It was clear to me that there may very well be rough seas ahead for Christopher, but with Dr. Lillehei in control, we could all survive somehow.

Christopher pulled through with flying colors and proved to us how strong he really was. He had to be a fighter to bounce back so quickly. We were so proud and even more eager to get him home this time. As usual, Big Chris headed back to New Jersey, but this time, to prepare again for the homecoming. He had been working two jobs for some extra cash to pay for his trips each weekend. We kept in touch daily by phone, and the days seemed never-ending to each of us. Another Friday evening arrived, and Big Chris drove up once again with my brother Paul to take us all home on Monday. We had decided to wait for a regular working day, just in case anything went wrong. We played it safe all the way. Since the arrangements had already been made, the hospital discharge went smoothly.

The ride home was long and even a little scary. We drove for seven hours in a van with our tiny baby hooked up to a portable oxygen tank. But for the first time in my life, I was fully responsible for my child. My prayers had been answered, and my baby was finally coming home. I was the luckiest person on earth and extremely proud to be a mom.

After seven long hours on the road, we pulled into our driveway, and our parents greeted us with a huge sign across the front porch reading, WELCOME HOME CHRISTOPHER. We brought him in and showed him around his new home. The nursery was ready and waiting for him. Big Chris could not wait to take the baby out into the yard to introduce him to our dog Duke. After everything settled down and our guests left, Big Chris and I sat on the couch together, holding our precious baby boy. We sat for several minutes, neither one of us saying a word. Finally, Big Chris looked at me, smiled, and said, "We did not make a very healthy baby, but he sure is a beautiful one." I will remember those words and that moment for as long as I live.

Chapter 6

Friends and Family

Several people came to visit during those first few days while we were all at home, and it was wonderful to "show off" our baby. Everyone had been praying for him for so long, and they all wanted to meet him. Christopher received enough clothes and stuffed animals to fill his bedroom, which was fine, because he slept with us anyway. One of the most special gifts I received was from a person who had never even met us. She was moved by Christopher's story due to her own experience with her premature son, and she knew exactly what I needed most of all. Her gift was composed of a bottle of tomato sauce, a box of spaghetti, and a handwritten poem:

Newborn Parents

A babe to hold and caress ever so gently,
is now in your arms.
Unique in his creation, individual in his personality.
Extra strength he has summoned
to make his way home.
Extra special he truly is indeed.
God gave him to you
For reasons you may never know.
You must have that needed stamina
to help this child grow.
You must have that demanded patience

to endure whatever passes on this son's
road he travels.
More so, you must have each other to create
a "family" to know,
A family of recognition of all strengths
and weaknesses.
A family of today and tomorrow's you share.
Life is not simple
But it can be full of love.
"Congratulations" on your dearest creation,
Newborn parents.

—Joylene Mierta

Joylene knew what I needed most of all: understanding and encouragement.

I learned quickly to enjoy the good times, the gentle smiles, the coos, and any scrap of sleep I could afford. The first night went well for Christopher. He did not even awaken during his first feeding, and of course, I did not mind when he woke up for the second one. It gave me another chance to see him. All of his medications, as well as his formula, went through the gastrostomy tube. I was used to setting up his feedings, so at first it did not seem that it was going to be a big deal, but reality set in rather quickly. Big Chris had to go to work in the morning, since he had missed so much time already. For the first time, I was to be truly alone with the baby, solely responsible for this fragile little life. One part of me wanted to sing with delight, while another part wanted to scream with fear.

After that first night, I never had more than a few minutes to think about anything. Special formula had to be prepared for the day, and medications needed to be drawn. The baby would be due for another feeding and then would need a bath. I would change the feeding tube dressing, then do his chest percussions and suctioning. In the middle of all this, the phone would ring, and it would be a call from the insurance company or a social worker. Each feeding lasted about forty-five minutes, and he had to be fed every two hours around the clock. I kept a schedule for the medications, and at night, I would set the alarm clock to wake me for the feedings. For the first few days, it didn't matter, because I never slept anyway. I was too afraid to close my eyes, for fear that he would vomit in his sleep or turn blue and stop breathing. Big Chris had to sleep, because he had to be at his first job at seven and would not return until seven o'clock in the evening. We were fortunate to have both of our families to help. Each day, they took turns preparing meals for us and visiting to provide us with moral support.

On October 27, 1986, Christopher went to Grandma Elsie's house for a family dinner. All of my brothers and sisters were there to meet him for the first time. He surprised us all by drinking the entire two ounces of his bottle by mouth. This was the first bottle he had ever finished completely by himself, and everyone commented on how healthy he looked. However, by the next morning, Christopher had become very irritable and fussy. His color had gone pale and bluish, and since I was never really sure about the parameters, I did not know whether to turn up his oxygen. I called the local pediatrician for an appointment, even though we had one scheduled later that week. I was uncomfortable waiting. Later that day, I packed Christopher up with his portable oxygen tank and went for our first pediatric visit.

The doctor came highly recommended by the hospital neonatologist, so I trusted that he must be competent and caring. However, I soon realized that not all physicians were inclined to give my baby special attention. This first visit was a disaster, and it should have been a warning sign for me to go elsewhere. The doctor knew all about Christopher ahead of time, yet we waited in a room full of sick children for over half an hour. When we finally went into an examination room, the doctor said that in many cases, babies come home from the hospital with oxygen, but they very seldom needed it. He told me that he would have my baby off oxygen and all medications in a couple of weeks. He dropped Christopher's thirty-calorie formula to twenty-four and told me to discontinue his diuretic. This doctor's words and actions puzzled me. Christopher was twenty-one inches long and weighed eight pounds, which meant he had gained eight ounces during his first week home. A gut feeling told me something was wrong, but I trusted the pediatrician. I assumed that he had spoken with the doctors in Boston, and that they must have agreed on these changes. At this point, I was still quite intimidated by medical personnel and would not dare question a doctor's authority or knowledge.

Within twenty-four hours, Christopher was admitted to the local hospital for possible aspiration pneumonia. He had retained fluid and gained an additional eight ounces. The doctor told me it was just a difference in scales, and that I had to try not to overreact. He also told me that ECMO was now in Christopher's past, that he was a regular kid, and that I must treat him that way. He put Christopher on antibiotics and changed his formula once more. I felt very uneasy about all of this, because my baby was far from an average infant. I decided to get in touch with Dr. Zitsman once again. Even though he was an hour away, I felt he must be willing to help us. Certainly, he would want to see Christopher, since he had operated on him the day he was born. It would also be a good opportunity for us to thank him personally for his lifesaving efforts.

Dr. Zitsman was thrilled to hear from us and asked us to come in as soon as possible. He admitted that it was rewarding for him to see his little patient, but upsetting to see Christopher with so many problems. Disagreeing with the pediatrician, Dr. Zitsman put Christopher back on a low-dose diuretic to help control his fluids and increased his reflux medication. He then scheduled a milk scan and an upper GI series for the following week.

From then on Christopher seemed to be getting stronger each day. He even began laughing and raising his head. Everyone was concerned about his development, but to me, he seemed to be just fine. I was told to expect delays because of his extensive illness, but that was the least of my worries. It was obvious from his behavior and mannerisms that he had not suffered severe brain damage.

The biggest problem for all of us was that he hardly ever slept. He was terribly uncomfortable and would often wake screaming with pain during his feedings. It was extremely frustrating, because I knew eating should be a natural comfort for a baby, but for Christopher it was agony. He would wake each morning gagging and choking, and nobody knew why or how to help him. I tried everything to keep him comfortable. His calories and nutrition were crucial to his recovery and growth, but caused so much discomfort. I wondered if he would ever eat like a "normal" baby.

By the time one month had passed, I was completely drained and exhausted. The days were long, and the nights seemed endless. Big Chris was hardly ever home, and the baby was a handful to manage on my own. Prescriptions had to be filled, insurance claims filed, and my phone never stopped ringing. I had visiting nurses often stopping by, and oxygen and feeding supplies were being delivered weekly. I never left the house, because I could not leave anyone with all the responsibility of such a fragile baby, though I never complained to anyone, because I felt in some way I had asked for all I got. My baby was hanging on the edge of death, yet I pleaded with the doctors to do everything they could and prayed that Christopher could endure the struggle.

Christopher was registered with the Board of Health due to the birth defect, so we were contacted by the local early intervention program and special child health services. Their goal was to assist us with any needs we might have and to evaluate Christopher's development. At that time, "fine motor skills" were the furthest things from my mind, and I had no clue what our needs were. For us, time was at a standstill; we survived moment-to-moment as the rest of the world went on its way.

Finally, the time came to take Christopher back to Boston for his follow-up appointment with Dr. Lillehei and Dr. Hershenson, the pulmonologist. It was mid-December and our son was almost four months old, yet it was the first trip to Boston that the three of us actually made together, and I was extremely grateful for that. Big Chris and I were both so thankful to have our baby, no matter how much work, time, or money he required. We were so proud to be his parents. Nothing could compare to the intense love we both had for our baby. When we arrived in the city, we made the hospital our very first stop. Everyone was so pleased to see him growing and thriving, and Christopher charmed them all with his warm smile and hearty giggles. He was quite the social babe.

The next morning, we had several appointments scheduled for Christopher to check his progress. Several tests were performed over our two-day visit. It never got any easier for me to hold down a screaming baby while he was being poked, probed, and turning blue. It would tear my heart out to see him in such pain, yet I always preferred being right there with him through each and every procedure than to leave him alone with strangers. It was lucky for me that at Boston Children's Hospital, parents were encouraged to stay with their baby.

Thankfully, it was an uneventful visit. Dr. Lillehei was pleased with Christopher's steady growth and progress, and we planned to keep everything the same and return in two months. He warned us that the winter months could be difficult, and that Christopher might need to be hospitalized for even a common cold. He explained that the first year might be full of ups and downs, and we should not be surprised if he became ill. I think the hardest part for all of us was that there was no way to predict his future. After all, he was their first survivor.

Chapter 7

Desperate Determination

Christopher, for some unknown reason, woke up each and every morning vomiting, coughing, and gagging. I would give him his reflux medications, wait thirty minutes, and then set up his feeding. I held him in my arms, and he sucked the pacifier while the formula was dripping into his G-tube. I tried to make the feedings as calm and normal as possible for both of us. At each feeding, he would spit up some of his formula. Not only was it messy, but I feared he would aspirate some of the formula and get sick again.

One morning, only three days before Christmas, while I was holding Christopher in my arms, he appeared to stop breathing and turned a light shade of blue. I had no idea what was happening, screaming for Big Chris to help. He entered the room and checked the oxygen tank and tubing, but both were working fine. He then grabbed the phone and frantically dialed 911. There was no obvious cause for what was occurring. I honestly thought the baby's heart had stopped, and that he might be dying in my arms. I examined his throat to see if he was choking, and something inside me told me to suction his airway. When I did this, he immediately began breathing and his color came back as well. By this time, the ambulance was at the door, ready to assist us. We had informed them ahead of time about the special needs of our baby, and they insisted that we take Christopher to the hospital to be examined by a physician. I went off in the ambulance while Big Chris went to work. Christopher's lungs sounded clear, but a chest X-ray and a blood sample were taken to be sure. Hours later, he was discharged, and I called my mother-in-law for a ride back to the house. Christopher and I were traumatized and exhausted, but finally going home. Later that evening, I prayed that the worst might be over for him, and that we could put the past behind us and move forward with our lives. The responsibility and daily care were more than enough for us, and now Christmas was quickly approaching. More than anything, I wanted Christmas to be a happy and fun-filled time for all of us. I struggled each day to make our lives as normal and routine as I could.

Our roles as parents were clearly defined right from the start. I would be the caretaker, and Big Chris would be the provider. Big Chris quickly learned that he would have to work hard if we were going to survive, and I learned that to be the mother of a sick baby was going to be a great responsibility. I had to coordinate all care and services for my child, as well as manage my household, so that our physical, emotional, and spiritual lives could run smoothly. The job was overwhelming at times, and to this day, my emotional state seems to be a reflection of my son's physical and emotional health.

Our first Christmas with Christopher was wonderfully exciting. His life was the most precious gift I could have ever received, and I cherished every moment with him. I never imagined being a mother could be so fulfilling and rewarding. Each milestone was such a major accomplishment for Christopher, and I was so proud and grateful for my little smooth sailor. At the same time, I felt sad and guilty for all the days we were apart, promising to never leave him again.

Christmas was a wonderful break and a blessing, but reality soon came crashing back. Only one short week later, on January 2, 1987, Christopher returned to the local emergency room for severe respiratory distress. It was the beginning of a very stormy winter for all of us.

Like before, the pediatrician told me that Christopher was fine, and I should just go home and relax. So for the next forty-eight hours, Christopher suffered at home until I insisted that the pediatrician meet us in the emergency room again. Christopher was gasping for each breath. His skin was mottled, and his eyes were swollen shut. He vomited all his formula and medications, so I could no longer manage him at home. He was admitted that afternoon to the special care room of pediatrics at our local hospital.

My baby intimidated the nurses, and it was clear that they had no special training to allow them to cope with an infant as medically fragile as Christopher. By law, he could not be in the nursery since he was no longer a newborn, so this was the only place for him. For the entire stay, I never left his side. I almost felt sorry for the nurses— some of whom were afraid to touch my son—but at the same time, I did not want him to be their guinea pig. I provided all of his care and spent any free time talking to the nurses about his history.

The pediatrician diagnosed Christopher with a virus. Each morning, he came in, saying that the infection just had to run its course. I disagreed with the diagnosis and kindly insisted that something more serious was wrong with the baby. I asked the pediatrician to contact Dr. Lillehei in Boston for some guidance or advice. If nothing else, I would feel a lot better. He replied that he had everything under control, and it was not necessary to bother a busy surgeon.

While amazingly calm on the outside, my insides were churning with fear and anger. Days went by with no positive changes. Christopher was extremely restless and uncomfortable. He never slept and continually cried, unless I held him under his arms and bounced him. When I did this, his color would significantly improve, and so would his temperament. So I bounced him to keep him comfortable day and night, until my arms were sore. The pediatrician almost laughed, remarking that the baby was just spoiled. I would have loved to punch him, but my arms were too tired. Five long days went by, and Christopher showed no improvement. I really wanted to believe the problem was viral, trying to put my trust in the professionals, but once again, my gut was telling me something was seriously wrong.

On January 9, my twenty-third birthday, Big Chris came up to the room with a single red rose he had purchased from the gift shop. He told me it was from Christopher for being the bravest and best mom ever. Later that evening, the doctor came in and told us to take the baby home, as he might recover better there. I agreed only because they were not doing anything for him at the hospital, and I had not slept in several days.

The next day, Christopher was no better, and perhaps even worse. Except now, I had to make all the decisions on my own again. If I called the doctor, he would think I was a neurotic mother, but if I did not, my baby would suffer. Christopher's color was poor—almost pale now—and he had diarrhea. He still vomited every feeding and just about all of his medications. Big Chris left for work, telling me to remain calm and to call him if it got worse. How much worse could it get?

I felt I had no choice but to call the pediatrician to inform him of the baby's worsening condition. He told me over the phone that it must be a secondary infection and to discontinue the Reglan. He felt it was irritating Christopher's stomach. It became clear to me that this man had no idea what was wrong with my son or how to treat him, and he refused to call the doctors in Boston.

I finally phoned Dr. Lillehei myself. He calmed me by supporting and verifying my concerns. He reminded me that I knew my child better than anyone, and said that if I was uncomfortable at home, I should go directly back to the hospital. He reminded me not to be a hero and to advocate for my son. He also agreed to speak with the local doctors.

It was an awful day and even a worse evening. Big Chris and I argued over Christopher's status. I was frustrated and overwhelmed with worry. I wanted my son in the hospital under some type of supervision. He thought we could handle it at home and feared they would only make things worse. I insisted there was something seriously wrong, but my husband was resistant to putting his child through unnecessary pain and testing.

Later that evening Big Chris went to sleep as usual, while I sat at the edge of the bed watching my baby struggle for each breath. I wondered how much his little heart could take. I pleaded with God for some relief for this child, and longed for a good night's sleep for my baby and me.

As the hours slowly passed, Christopher's already frail body grew even weaker. My arms throbbed from bouncing him, and my heart ached from watching him suffer. By two o'clock in the morning, I could not bear it any more. Hysterically, I woke my husband and declared that we needed to go to the hospital. I was still extremely upset as I called the pediatrician and told him we were on our way to Mercer Medical Center. He told us he would meet us in the emergency room.

My husband and I argued all the way to the hospital. He thought I was overreacting and we could have waited until the morning, while I felt that by morning it might be too late. I feared for Christopher's life, worried that his little heart would stop, that it would be all over, and it would be my fault. I was totally responsible for his survival.

In the ten minutes it took us to arrive, we realized we probably should have called an ambulance. Christopher was blue and swollen with fluid. They put him on five liters of oxygen and gave him an injection of Lasix. I could not keep myself from questioning their expertise, and in my mind, I never trusted their decisions.

At four o'clock, our pediatrician finally arrived. He stood at the foot of the crib and told us to keep him comfortable. His words seemed so distant and heartless I could not help but wonder what his thoughts were. Maybe he did not expect our baby to survive. Maybe he thought it was all just a waste of time. I wished he would say something or send us somewhere else. My child's life was at stake, and that was all that mattered.

Chapter 8

Am I Losing My Mind?

There I sat, alone and afraid with my sick baby. Big Chris left for work, and none of our family or friends knew we were back in the hospital. The doctors had no idea what to do for us. I felt as though we were being punished for something. I wished more than anything to get back to Boston, where they would know what to do and I could trust them wholeheartedly. At our local hospital, we were not taken seriously, and even worse, often avoided. What my ears and eyes witnessed at that institution was unbelievable, and I wanted my baby out of there. We lived only an hour away from Philly, so I suggested the Children's Hospital of Philadelphia. My physician claimed they had no beds available, and felt Christopher would be fine in a few days. So for five agonizing days, I watched my baby suffer. I was going out of my mind with fear. He was extremely sick, and nobody seemed to be taking his illness seriously.

One morning I worked up enough courage to ask about the premature baby who had been in the next bed a few nights ago. They reluctantly told me that she had died from heart failure as a result of a severe stomach virus. I started losing my cool at that point. For four days, I watched the nurses play with her and joke about her as if she was their play toy, rather than a sick baby. That little girl supposedly had the same virus as Christopher, and now she was dead. When the doctors came around that morning, I insisted that something was very wrong. I also accused them of neglecting my son and treating his life too casually.

They both looked at me with amazement. Until then, I was nothing but kind, considerate, and agreeable with them. I was truly at my breaking point when I demanded better care. I felt as if my child's life was slipping away before my eyes. Minute by minute, Christopher was getting visibly worse. I called my husband and had him come back to the hospital. He called both of our parents, who also came up immediately. It seemed as if everyone except for the doctors understood how ill he was. One of the nurses agreed that we should transport him elsewhere, but we were running out of time. I refused to leave him for a moment and pleaded for someone to call Boston Children's for advice and guidance. Again, they refused to do so, claiming to have everything under control.

The pediatrician and neonatologist finally discussed intubating the baby. Unbelievably, I was asking them to put my son on a ventilator. I knew he was too weak to survive on his own, and he had suffered enough. They waited about an hour to come back to the room, and when they did it was almost too late. I cried out, "My baby is going to die if you don't do something quick!" A hasty decision was made, and now it was an emergency situation.

Throwing my hands into the air, I ran out of the room. I honestly thought my baby was dying in my arms, that his heart was going to quit, and at last they believed me. I lost control of myself for the first time since he was born. I could not be strong anymore. Big Chris stayed in the room for the procedure and held down his own son while they inserted a breathing tube. I was out in the hallway, punching doors and windows out of frustration, fear, and exhaustion. Nobody even attempted to console me or come near me. They were all clueless and maybe even guilty. I waited for a sign that the ventilator was on and working. It was actually a relief this time to see him on life support and resting comfortably. That poor baby had to work too hard and fight too long. I was furious with the doctors and could not look at either one of them. They, too, were speechless.

As soon as my baby was stabilized, I ran down to the nurse's station and called Dr. Lillehei. I knew there was not much he could do long distance, but I just had to talk to him to convey my concerns. He agreed that to have the baby transported elsewhere would be a good idea for both of us. As I was speaking to him, I remembered Children's Hospital of Philadelphia. With his approval for the move, I hung up and went back to see Christopher.

I was determined to have him out of there that afternoon, especially when I saw the ventilator settings, which had never been that high before. Christopher was not breathing at all on his own. He was heavily sedated and failing quickly. I had to do everything in my power to get him out fast. Both doctors told me he was too sick to be transported, and that I was being unrealistic by trying to do so. They tried to make me feel guilty for wanting to move my son. At that point, I demanded they call St. Christopher's Hospital, and request an immediate transfer. I refused to take no for an answer.

Reluctantly, they agreed, and within the hour, the transport team was on their way. I spoke with them over the phone and made all the arrangements myself. From our simple five-minute telephone conversation, I knew that competent help was on its way. I went back to Christopher, held his little hand, and thanked God for another chance.

In the meantime, the doctor started a blood transfusion, to which Christopher had a severe reaction. He became as white as his sheets, and his blood oxygen levels dropped significantly. I asked them to stop guessing, keep him comfortable, and wait for the transport team.

It was a good thing our mothers were there with us, because we needed all the support we could get. The intense emotional highs and lows were too much to handle alone. We were not giving much support for each other anymore. We tended to become so wrapped up in our own feelings during the times of crisis. It was never until much later that we could look back and process what happened, or even feel emotion or compassion for each other. Our only concern was the health of our son and getting through another day together.

Chapter 9

Back to Boston

Two hours later, a male and a female physician arrived from Philadelphia. They assured us we had made the right decision and told us that everything would be okay. They were very comfortable about the transport and included us from the start with all decisions regarding Christopher's care. They first made several changes to the ventilator settings, reduced the sedative, and lowered the amount of oxygen he was receiving. His color improved straightaway, and so did our morale. We felt like he was in good hands, and once again, our confidence was restored. The doctors stayed with us and listened to all our questions and concerns. They were familiar with ECMO and were pleased to see Christopher thriving. We talked for a long time while they waited to see how he would react to the changes. They made several phone calls back to the hospital to prepare for his arrival.

The conduct of these doctors from Philadelphia stood in stark contrast to the hellish place we had just come from. Rather than gambling on our son's life and keeping us in the dark, they validated our concerns and valued our input. They knew that as parents, we had an intimate knowledge of Christopher's medical history and his behaviors, and we deserved a say in his care.

By early evening, we were happy to be on our way to St. Christopher's Hospital in Philadelphia. Christopher traveled by ambulance, and we followed in our own car. We laughed and cried the whole way. Christopher was admitted directly into the intensive care unit when we arrived. I was glad to have him there, but I still wished he had been in Boston instead. We had come to trust the team in Boston and had had so many poor experiences elsewhere that it was difficult to feel comfortable leaving Christopher in anyone else's care. Here in Philadelphia, he had a whole new team of people and unfamiliar surroundings. I was only able to see Christopher for a few minutes the first evening because they did not allow parents to stay through the night. Big Chris went home while a guard escorted me to another building with lodgings for me. Within four nights in the intensive care unit, Christopher improved enough to be transferred to a medical floor. He seemed to be stronger and happier than ever, and as energetic as any other five-month-old baby. As usual, his quick recovery took everyone by surprise. His spirit always had an unusual resilience and an ability to bounce back from suffering.

We had been given new hope and were returned home with medication and breathing treatments. The prompt and knowledgeable attention that Christopher had received from the physicians in Philadelphia lifted our spirits, but it was not to last.

Only one week later, we were off to Philadelphia again. This time, I went directly to the hospital's emergency room. Christopher's eyes were puffy, and he was clearly in respiratory distress. We did not know it then, but we eventually learned that when Christopher showed these signs, it was indicative of congestive heart failure. He was given extra diuretics and admitted to the intensive care unit again for observations. In the meantime, I called Dr. Lillehei to express my concerns about the fluid build-up. He recommended that Christopher be stabilized and brought back to Boston for a possible heart catheterization. We did just that. He was discharged from the ICU, and Big Chris and I drove to Boston through sleet and snow to get some answers and peace of mind. We were greeted with open arms, and this time, Christopher was admitted to the toddler room. Now he was one of the big boys.

Big Chris took the subway to the airport and caught the first plane back to New Jersey so that he could go to work the next day. I met with a cardiologist the next morning. He was kind, gentle, and sincere. We discussed the problem Christopher was having with fluid accumulation, and he ordered an echocardiogram to be done the following morning. He chose to avoid a heart catheterization at that time. The ECG was performed under mild sedation, and the cardiologist came to me immediately with the results. As he stroked Christopher's little arm, he explained that my baby had an atrial septal defect. In simpler terms, he now had a hole in the wall, separating the upper chambers of his heart, causing insufficient blood oxygenation. This defect, which is usually present at birth, may have developed as a result of Christopher's other complications. I could not believe it. He was born with a hole in his diaphragm and now a hole in his heart. The cardiologist calmly and directly explained to me that he would increase the diuretics to three times a day. There was a good chance the defect might close on its own if we could eliminate excess fluid, so that his heart would not have to pump so hard. Other tests were performed which confirmed the need for Digoxin, a medication to strengthen and regulate his heartbeat.

While hospitalized, Christopher began having viral symptoms once again. They put him in a mist tent and began nebulizer treatments for his wheezing, along with physical therapy on his chest and suctioning every four hours. This went on for five more days. Dr. Lillehei informed us he would keep Christopher for another week until he was strong and well, which was fine with me. I felt much safer and more secure being right where I was.

Each evening, I called Big Chris to give him a report about the day. It was not easy being apart, but we both knew I had no choice but to stay in Boston. For now, it was the best thing to do. The phone calls were difficult; it was always upsetting to me to pass along bad news. I often waited until I was feeling good before I called home, especially when it was a call to the grandparents. Christopher's condition was hard enough for me to handle, and I did not like to get them upset. I often tried to sugarcoat the problems while keeping everyone informed. I never wanted anyone to feel sorry for me; I wanted them to put all their energy into positive prayer and wishes for Christopher. I trusted the doctors' every decision in Boston.

Within two days, a chest X-ray indicated decreased lung size on the left side. Although there was great concern about putting Christopher through an operation due to the precarious state of his health, Dr. Lillehei felt the best course was to attempt to re-inflate the collapsed lung. He performed a bronchoscopy under general anesthesia and attempted the procedure. Unfortunately, he was unsuccessful, and concluded that Christopher's lung must have been that way for some time. However, Christopher once again proved to all of us how strong he really was. In spite of the impaired lung, a week later, he was ready to go home. Big Chris flew up to meet us, and we all drove home together. Luckily, the weather cooperated, and the drive home went smoothly for once.

I thought for sure this trip from Boston would be the last. It just had to be. What more could go wrong? I made an appointment with a new pediatrician for the very next day. She was very interested in caring for my baby and had experience in neo-natal intensive care. More importantly, she understood the seriousness of Christopher's condition and the importance of communicating with the doctors in Boston.

Chapter 10

All Out Of Tears

Christopher was now six months old and weighed only thirteen pounds. His height and weight were in the fifth percentile, while his head circumference was in the ninety-fifth. Christopher's pediatrician was amazed at his alertness and sociability. She promised to play an active role in his recovery. She was encouraging and supportive, yet warned that she was no hero. That was all I wanted to hear from her.

She examined Christopher while he was in good health, but heard some wheezing in his chest. She prescribed nebulizer treatments and a mist tent for our home to get him through the winter months. I trusted her decision and left with a good feeling this time.

Within a week, Christopher woke up with puffy eyes again. I could hardly believe it was happening. I was sure we had this all under control; I was feeling so defeated. This time we knew our baby was in congestive heart failure, and within hours, he began experiencing severe respiratory distress.

Alone once again, I put my blue-skinned infant in the car and reluctantly drove back to the local emergency room. The doctors thankfully asked me what to do to treat him. I told them to give him an intramuscular dose of Lasix and he would be fine, so they did. One doctor jokingly offered me a job upstairs in the nursery. He called Dr. Flores, and she increased his daily Lasix. The very next day, I went to her office because he was still retaining fluid. This seemed impossible, since he vomited most of what I fed him. I had no idea what he actually retained. She also increased his Digoxin and then sent us home.

Within only eighteen hours, I was rushing my baby back to the ER for the same reason. Every time, I feared it would be the last. I could not imagine how much more this little guy could take. When Christopher was well, he was great. When he was sick, it was always to an alarming degree. Even a simple ear infection was enough to send him into heart failure. He was hospitalized and given two large doses of Lasix just to stabilize him. As usual, blood gasses tests and chest x-rays were performed. His electrolytes were off, so he stayed the night for more testing.

He was discharged, but was not well. I was petrified to be home with my own son. He was so unstable and unhappy, and I was the one responsible for every breath of life. It completely drained me of all energy and emotion. I did not cry anymore; I just became angry. I was angry with the doctors and my husband, angry that we had to be so far away from Boston, and angry with God for allowing this to go on for so long. There were too many unanswered questions and uncertainties. My baby's tender smile was the only thing that kept me going.

Over the next several days I remained in contact with the doctors from Boston. Each day, Christopher grew weaker and weaker. I refused to go back to Mercer Hospital ever again and watch them stab and poke my baby. Somehow, I convinced Dr. Lillehei to send a transport team back for Christopher. There was no way we would have made the six-hour drive this time. Our new pediatrician agreed and made the arrangements for us. He was admitted to Mercer Hospital in order to do the transport.

After only three weeks at home, Christopher was on his way back to Boston. A plane arrived once again with an amazing transport team, and within hours, they were on their way back to Boston. I had taken a separate flight from Philadelphia and arrived much later that evening. I really thought my baby was dying, and I knew I could never accept this if it happened in New Jersey. I found great comfort in going back to be in Dr. Lillehei's care. I traveled alone and actually preferred it that way. I did not want to feel like I had to entertain anyone. All of my attention was on Christopher, and alone I could stay by his side twenty-four hours a day. I felt relatively at ease in Boston, and I trusted whatever they said to be true. Elaine was working that evening, so I was sure to get some sleep. We chatted for a while, then I went to the parents' lounge, found a couch, and fell asleep.

By morning, Christopher was happy and smiling once again, as if nothing had ever happened. It was amazing how quickly he could recover after a hefty dose of Lasix. Dr. Lillehei felt we should stay for a while so that he could watch and make sure he made steady progress. He thought he would survive, but it might be a much slower process than anticipated. I agreed to stay as long as necessary to ensure the well-being of my child, but he was also concerned for my long-distance marriage. He really thought our local children's hospital would have worked for us so we could have been closer to home. I explained to him that we both agreed that Christopher belonged in Boston. Otherwise, the stress and worry were too overwhelming. We did what was best for our son, and put everything else on hold. Besides, I had lost touch with the outside world months ago. I lived each day inside the hospital walls beside my baby. At least, in the hospital I was never lonely or depressed. There were plenty of other parents around, and we all helped each other cope. Here I could just be a mom and enjoy my son. I was only consulted on medical decisions; I did not have to make them.

Calling home was still the most difficult time of the day. Unless there was significant change, there wasn't much to say. Everyone wanted to know when we would come home, but I had no idea and I did not care.

My weakest moments came at night, when I was alone in my room. I was staying in an old empty nursing dorm across the street, because it was only fifteen dollars a night. I would walk over after the eleven o'clock shift change, so that I knew who would be caring for him through the night. By the time I reached my room, the tears would be flowing and I would simply fall to the cot in exhaustion and cry myself to sleep. Somehow, in the morning, I would jump back up with a smile, ready to face the challenges of a new day.

Chapter 11

Craving Normalcy

Every day was some sort of challenge, like the head ultrasound that was scheduled as part of a routine followed on all ECMO patients. Christopher was given chloral hydrate to make him sleepy, and off we went for the test. I was sure everything would be normal. I was relaxed and at ease, while I held my baby's hand during the procedure. As usual, I asked the technologist how things looked, and he hesitated before he replied. The baby had excess fluid in the ventricles of his brain. I sat there, stunned at his reply, but grateful for his honesty. Besides, if he was telling me about it, how bad could it be? Well, the wheels started turning in my head. Is this the way life was going to be from now on? A neurologist was consulted immediately, and he felt the amount of fluid was slight at the time. Only if it should build up would he consider a shunt to drain the fluid off the brain.

My concern was having another problem to worry about every day of his life. I was told to have his head measured regularly, to keep a chart of the findings, and to monitor his behavior for drastic changes. I accepted the news as part of the side effects of ECMO. There was no reason to waste energy on worrying about what issues might arise in the future. We had plenty of issues to overcome at the present time.

We returned to his room to find a note taped to the bedside table. It read: "Your sister Gina had a baby boy!" I was excited and crushed at the same time. I wanted to be home with my family and to share in that special event of a normal birth experience. I began feeling sorry for myself and longed for some normalcy in my life.

When this all began after Christopher's birth, I never imagined we would still be going through such devastation seven months later. I felt incredibly lonely and detached from everyone I loved. Every day I alternated between celebrating my son's life and fearing his death.

I called home to my husband and told him he needed to come to Boston right away. Christopher's heart catheterization was going to be done the following morning, and I was not strong enough to experience it alone this time. The procedure itself was not the problem. It was the results I feared the most.

The cardiologist explained that we would have accurate measures of Christopher's pulmonary hypertension (the pressure through the pulmonary arteries). It was necessary at this point to know exactly why Christopher suffered from congestive heart failure, and if medical management would be enough.

Big Chris arrived just as the baby came back from the test. Christopher was sleeping comfortably, which gave us a moment to be alone together. We wanted so much to hold him in our arms and cherish the moment before the doctors came in with the results. We knew it could be our final moments of hope, but Christopher had to remain flat on the bed, so we sat beside him stoking his arms and legs. Neither one of us could take our eyes nor hands off of him.

Dr. Hershenson and the cardiologist entered the room together, and the tears began streaming down my face before either man could speak. The somber look on their faces told me everything. The doctors were both surprised by the degree of pulmonary hypertension they had discovered. It was much greater than they had anticipated. Medications and supplemental oxygen would not be enough, and they feared that this could worsen as he grew. The cardiologist reminded us that Christopher was unique in that there was no other survivor ahead of him for comparison. We would just have to wait and see. He went on to explain how children born with a restricted pulmonary artery rarely live for long. He gave our son a fifty percent chance of living beyond age two.

When the doctors finished speaking, I stood up and looked at my precious child lying there in his yellow hospital gown. He smiled innocently at me, as if to say it would be all right. I wept in disbelief that his life could be taken away. Why now, when he had come so far and fought so hard? The doctors stood beside us in full support, understanding our grief. All I could do was thank them for their unfailing dedication.

Dr. Lillehei was surprised at the findings as well, and said that no other ECMO survivor had displayed such high pressures. Only time would tell if his body would grow and adapt enough to sustain his life. He apologized for the bad news and promised to stay committed to Christopher and his future. He promised he was not giving up, and his words gave me hope. He also reminded us that each day brought us closer to new discoveries, and that one day, Christopher might be a candidate for a lung transplant. I asked him if he had discussed his case with other physicians around the country, thinking someone might have a magical answer to save my son's life. I was willing to do anything for my baby, so I expressed whatever thought came to my head. He said he had been in contact with several colleagues throughout the United States. He was one step ahead of us at all times. I asked him if I should have hope or if I should be prepared for the worst. He left the room with a command and a promise: "Do not ever give up hope on Christopher. I always have something up my sleeve." I believed those words with all my heart and soul.

Chapter 12

An Unexpected Solution

Dr. Hershenson, the pulmonologist, stayed in the room for a while, talking to Big Chris and me about Christopher. He was also not ready to give up on his star patient. We were discussing Christopher's breathing difficulties when, out of the blue, my husband asked if an iron lung would help. *An iron lung?* I thought. *Like the ones that were used for polio patients years ago?* I was shocked at his idea and wondered where in the world it had come from. Big Chris had never said much of anything to the doctors before, usually letting me do all the talking. More surprising, still, was the doctor's positive reaction to the idea.

After briefly considering the idea, Dr. Hershenson became excited and began plans to have Christopher do a trial run in an iron lung. I was thrilled to think there might be a solution after all. Within forty-eight hours, Christopher was back in the ICU for his first night in the negative pressure ventilator. He was sedated enough to tolerate the machine, then his body was placed inside the big glass tank with only his head remaining outside. The machine looked archaic to me. I was excited and nervous at the same time. Everyone around us was optimistic and interested to see whether it would work. The negative pressure on his chest allowed his body to rest while the machine did the work, thus easing the overload on his heart and lowering the pressures in his pulmonary arteries.

Christopher was monitored very closely throughout the night. Unfortunately, Big Chris had to go home and could not be there to witness his brilliant idea at work. I was glad to have my mother stay with me for a few days to keep me company and give me moral support. Christopher surprised me and tolerated the ventilator very well. The rhythmic motion and hum of the motor soothed him, and he seemed more peaceful than usual. But in the morning, the results were questionable. Christopher's fluid output was low, as usual, and he required additional Lasix. The doctors decided to continue the iron lung treatment for one week before evaluating the benefits. The nurses weighed each diaper, closely monitoring his fluid output, and adjusted the diuretics accordingly. Each night, he was sedated and placed in the huge green tank. He was still fed continuously through the gastrostomy tube, so there was a concern about vomiting, but otherwise, the days and nights were fairly uneventful. Christopher would wake up energized and ready to play. I would bathe him and dress him in big-boy clothes. His crib was full of toys and books, but he enjoyed interacting with people the most. I would put him in a walker with a long oxygen tube, and off he would go around the ICU. He was the picture of health to those who did not know him, and became very popular with all the nurses and therapists in the unit.

After a week in the iron lung, we all decided it was having a positive effect on Christopher and that he should continue using it indefinitely, as long as he was doing well. I was prepared to stay in Boston for another week or two. My mother went back to New Jersey, and Big Chris's mom came up to spend a few days with us. She was astonished at how wonderful Christopher looked and behaved. He could sit up and play peek-a-boo like a normal seven-month-old. We all enjoyed his health and happiness and looked forward to the day when he could come home again. Just the same, I did not want to rush things this time, because I wanted this trip to Boston to be the last.

An ECG revealed slight improvement in Christopher's arterial pressures. In addition, a lung scan showed increased airflow into the impaired left lung. Christopher was looking better than ever. Dr. Hershenson decided it would be best for him to stay at Boston Children's Hospital for a couple of weeks, then go home with a portable iron lung. This was fantastic news. I never bothered asking about long-range possibilities, but took one day at a time, remembering that Christopher was growing stronger every day.

During that four-week visit, Big Chris and I started growing farther apart. For me, Boston was home. It was where I felt safe and comfortable, and where I could freely and fully enjoy being a new mother. The hospital staff became my extended family and greatest support. I grew close to several other families, who were in similar situations, and I could not have cared less about the world outside. I lived there 24/7, while Big Chris was just a visitor on the weekend. My priority was to spend quality time with the baby. I cherished our time together, never able to shrug off the fear that Christopher could be taken away at any time.

Chapter 13

Are We Losing the Battle?

On a sunny April Sunday, we drove our fragile baby home to New Jersey, hoping as usual that it was the last time. I knew it was not going to be easy, but at least we were going to have nursing help at night. All of the arrangements had been made in advance for an RN to work in our home, starting the first night. Up until this time, we did not qualify for nursing or any assistance, but now, due to the iron lung and our dwindling funds, we qualified for a Medicaid Model Waiver. We received approval for one eight-hour shift of nursing coverage per day, without which we could not have brought our baby home. We needed to be home and together once again.

Christopher had been hospitalized for a month this time, so being home was a big adjustment. I showed the nurse how to use the iron lung and gave her a brief overview of his history. She seemed quite confident about caring for Christopher, but I insisted that she wake me with any questions or concerns, even though I did not sleep a wink the first couple of nights. It was very awkward having a stranger in our tiny two-bedroom home, caring for my baby. She came in at 11 p.m. and left at 7 a.m., so there was not much time to get to know her. I could only hope that she would follow the instructions from the discharge papers accurately.

This time, I was handling things differently. I was determined to stay at home with Christopher and keep him out of the hospital for a while. I weighed every diaper to measure his output and regulated his Lasix accordingly. I knew it would not take much to tip him over the edge into heart failure. I was tired of feeling like a failure as a parent and strived to do my best for him.

It's difficult to describe the sadness I felt when the symptoms began all over again. After only three short days at home, Christopher went into congestive heart failure. I had no choice but to rush him to a hospital in Philadelphia. I called my mother-in-law to come along, knowing he would get worse on the hour car ride to Pennsylvania. The hardest part was knowing what Christopher would have to face at the hospital. Each time was practically a fresh start; all new faces and a new team of people to explain things to all over again. I hoped and prayed they could understand the seriousness of our situation.

We arrived early in the afternoon at the emergency room for what turned out to be a disaster. Several residents made numerous attempts to draw blood from my blue baby. When one of them was finally successful, he dropped the sample on the floor. A chest X-ray was taken, but the file containing Christopher's old X-rays could not be found to make comparisons. A nurse then dropped his portable oxygen tank, sending water down the tube and up his nose, choking him. Through all of this, I remained fairly calm, remembering that they saw him as just another kid. It was my job to be an advocate for him, and by doing that, I had learned to put my baby's needs first. But I had also learned I did not have to worry about being nice or hurting someone's feelings when my child's life was at stake. If they did not know I was drained and exhausted from the last eight months, sometimes it was my responsibility to let them know.

It felt as though all the good times had been erased, and we were back to square one. Christopher was admitted to the ICU for three days, with iron lung and all. Big Chris had sold our small sedan and bought a truck large enough to transport the ventilator home from Boston. Now he brought it to Philadelphia as well. A couple of injections of diuretics and Christopher was happy and playing again. I pleaded with them to discharge him directly from the intensive care unit to avoid the medical floor and further germ exposure. They reluctantly agreed with my request.

But this time, we did not go straight home. I thought perhaps he was allergic to something at our house and that was why he kept getting sick. I was willing to try anything which might help my baby to stay well. I moved into my mother's house, which was only five minutes away, just to see if it would make a difference. I wanted a solution to his suffering and pain.

In spite of the change in houses, Christopher was only out of the hospital for five days when he went into heart failure again. We were forced once more to decide where we would go this time. Although Big Chris was hesitant, we both agreed to get Christopher back to Boston Children's Hospital. But how? He was wheezing, puffy, and now vomiting as well. His temperature was climbing, and he did not respond to the second dose of Lasix. I began calling several medical flight agencies, feeling in my gut that he would not survive the six-hour drive.

Big Chris and I argued back and forth all through the night. We agonized further about the decision, considering the distance we would have to travel, and how else to get help. I held Christopher under the arms and bounced him up and down so he could breathe, then Big Chris would take a turn. We screamed at each other and cried as our baby deteriorated rapidly. At this point, we had no stamina or energy left to care for our own child. As the sun came up, we made a hasty decision to get into the truck, turn up the oxygen, and drive to Boston. We never even called ahead, fearing they would discourage the trip. It was our choice for Christopher. After a horrifying six-hour drive, thinking of all the hospitals we were passing along the way, we arrived at the emergency room of Boston Children's Hospital for the eighth time that year.

Christopher was in severe respiratory failure, and we were tremendously relieved to be there. If there was to be bad news, I knew in my heart I could only accept it from Dr. Lillehei. My husband never even parked the car this time. He handed me my luggage, kissed us goodbye, wished us well, and drove back home alone. It was April 27, 1987, our second anniversary.

Chapter 14

The Prayer

The emergency room staff was shocked by the baby's fragile condition. They phoned Dr. Lillehei to let him know we had arrived. He made arrangements for a bed in the ICU.

Christopher was not responding to the diuretics as he normally did, and his oxygen saturation level dropped throughout the evening. It was lucky for me that Elaine was scheduled to start work at eleven and would be with Christopher all night. This meant I could go off to the parent room for some rest, knowing she would wake me if he deteriorated. I would certainly not get any sleep, but at least I could step away to get a break from it all. I needed time alone to process what was going on. I could not comprehend how this could all be happening to him again.

My greatest worry was whether Christopher could keep on fighting. I worried about his potential quality of life, growing up dependent on medical technology for survival. Anxious about the long-term effects of all the drugs and treatments, I began to question it all. Even if he *could* win this battle, *should* he? The stress was overwhelming, almost to the point that I could not think clearly. I wondered if there was anyone who might understand. My concern was that if I let go, they all might stop trying so hard. I thought it was up to me, that in some way, I had the power to keep everyone fighting. That night, alone in my room, I got down on my knees, prayed, and cried out to God like never before: "Dear Lord, give me the courage to put my trust in you. Please give me the strength to face the coming day. Fill my soul with wisdom and understanding, and fill my heart with peace. Free Christopher from his pain and suffering. I sit by his side and hold him down while he is stabbed, poked, and probed over and over again, and the pain in my heart is more than I can bear. I am done fighting, and I believe he is too. I surrender his life to you! Amen."

At five o'clock in the morning, there was a knock at the door. It was Elaine, who had come to tell me that Christopher was not doing very well. I rushed to his side and asked for her advice. "Please be perfectly honest with me," I said. "Is he ever going to be okay?" Elaine replied, "I can tell you that it does not look good. He is not responding the way he usually does, but as long as there is breath, there is life. As long as there is life, there is hope!" I told her how I was feeling, and that I expected bad news in this visit. I told her how afraid I was to lose him, but how exhausted I was from the care and worry. She was incredibly supportive and understanding of my feelings. She kept apologizing for the situation and asked how she could help. I wanted her to tell me how to feel or what to think, because I was thoroughly confused at the time.

As I spent countless nights in the parent room, I witnessed many families come and go. I shared stories with those families and their children. Some entered in critical condition and left the hospital in a day or two, miraculously cured. Others had been coming in and out of the hospital for years, and still, there were others whose loved ones died. I wondered where we would fit into the picture. I wanted answers, a sign from God that everything would be okay.

Christopher woke up and smiled a peaceful smile. His eyelids were almost swollen shut, and his frail body was working hard for each breath. I picked him up and held him close to me. I could feel his heart pounding and could visualize each breath of air as it filled his lungs. More than anything, I wanted him to be comfortable. I was so in love with this little boy, and I craved a day that I would not have to worry about his suffering. I rocked him and sang to him all day long, as streams of physicians filed in to examine him. I decided not to ask many questions this time and to just accept what they had to say.

Christopher remained the same for the next few days. His fluid levels and electrolytes were watched very closely. The iron lung was brought back in, and the same routine was started all over again. During that week, Elaine invited me to dinner at a local restaurant. I asked her if she would please make Christopher a christening outfit, because I wanted him baptized in our church when he got home. I never told her the real reason I wanted it. If he were to die, I wanted him to be buried wearing something special. I thought that I should start preparing for the worst, so that I could handle it when it happened.

By the time Big Chris arrived that weekend, the baby had begun showing slight improvement. Big Chris started asking questions about coming home again, while I thought it was time we just moved to Boston. Dr. Lillehei suggested we take one day at a time for a while. This time, he was concerned for Christopher's electrolyte levels. For some reason, he could not raise his chloride level, and he felt that this might be the reason he was retaining fluid. Dr. Hershenson suggested an oral dose of ammonium chloride along with potassium chloride to see if that would balance things out. Within days, his chloride levels rose and the fluid was released. Christopher was still on high doses of diuretics and was given only minimal fluid in order to survive, but for now it was working. He made slow and steady progress over the next few weeks. He began to sit up, talk, and cruise in his walker like a normal baby.

That first year of his life was extremely difficult for all of us. Our medical bills kept climbing, our family life was hectic, and the pain and heartache for our child consumed us. All-in-all, Christopher was hospitalized eighteen times for his various problems. Most of it was behind us, yet Big Chris and I still faced the massive responsibility of caring for a fragile baby at home. We were physically and emotionally exhausted, feeling alone and helpless.

Chapter 15

Happy Birthday Christopher

Christopher was on an uphill climb, but he was happier than ever and actually enjoyed living at Boston Children's Hospital. He had my undivided attention, and we spent our days reading books, singing songs, and playing together. He did not look like he belonged in an intensive care unit, but that is where he stayed for four weeks.

I concentrated on enjoying his good health and maintaining a positive attitude. As the weeks slowly passed, I began preparing myself for the trip back home to New Jersey. Accepting the fact that we would probably be back, I did not say farewell this time. The doctors had warned that it could be years before Christopher would eat and breathe on his own. As I had heard often during Christopher's first year, "only time would tell."

I accepted these words with gratitude as I learned to develop reasonable expectations for Christopher's recovery. On the morning of Memorial Day, May 27, Christopher was discharged from the ICU.

Once home, we continued with the iron lung and nursing through the night. Each morning, I would hesitate to look at Christopher, fearing the dreaded cyanosis and swollen eyes. In spite of my uncertainties, the good days finally began to outnumber the bad. Christopher sailed through his first week back home without complications. Family members and friends organized a "Baby Christopher Fund" to help defray our medical expenses, and prayer chains continued throughout New Jersey.

To our surprise, Christopher remained home for eight weeks without any major complications. On July 21, we drove back to Boston for a regular follow-up appointment. During that four-day visit, Christopher was tested from head to toe, and overall, the doctors were pleased and optimistic. They were most impressed by his activity level and outgoing personality. Though no long-term expectations were discussed, their hope was that someday he would outgrow all of it. This was our first trip to Boston that was not met with tragedy. We went home excited and eager to make plans for his first birthday party and his christening. We wanted it to be a huge celebration and a show of gratitude for all who had helped us through the most difficult year of our lives.

On August 21, 1987, our entire family celebrated Christopher's first birthday. As he was being baptized, I looked down at his pudgy cheeks and tender smile, and prayed that we could all move forward and that the worst was behind him. His birthday was a time to celebrate his life and a future. God filled my heart with more joy and peace than I could understand. My faith in him increased from that day on, and a hunger for more knowledge grew inside of me. Though I never thought of myself as a religious person, I knew that God had heard my prayers and the prayers of my family, friends, and neighbors. Christopher never went into congestive heart failure or the intensive care unit again.

Bringing Things Up-to-Date

One to two years old

Remarkably, Christopher began walking at fourteen months. He enjoyed attending weekly early intervention classes for speech and physical therapy. The iron lung was discontinued at fifteen months, but the oxygen and feeding tube remained. His GI problems continued, and he often experienced high fevers for no discernible reason. Christopher's smile and zest for life kept me going during the hardest days.

Caring for my son consumed every minute of every day. I rarely left home and still panicked with each cold and fever. He was my world, and I was afraid that I could still lose him at any moment. I knew that each day, home meant he was getting stronger, and I felt we were buying time for the future. Each day brought new advances in medicine and new hope.

Two to three years old

For the first time ever, we were told to expect our son to live a full and productive life. Christopher's pulmonary arterial pressure had improved to the point where he could forego oxygen during waking hours. It took him a long time to become comfortable without the oxygen cannula taped to his face, and he still required nutrition by feeding tube most of the time, but I could finally relax a little and bring him into the world with me. One of the greatest thrills for me was the first time he joined me on an errand to the grocery store. So many times before, I wandered through the aisles alone, and I wanted to shout at others that I was a mother, and that one day, my baby would be with me. Now, to my delight, he finally was.

I remained in close contact with the doctors in Boston, because they were the only ones who understood that Christopher's problems would not be totally resolved for a long time. I was trained as a support parent and began helping other families whose children had similar medical needs. It was good to know I was not alone, and that my experience could be used to benefit someone else.

Three to four years old

Shortly after Christopher's third birthday, his G-tube was removed, marking the first time since birth that he was truly tube-free. He was becoming a regular kid: a happy and energetic toddler who enjoyed everything other than being separated from me. I enjoyed being with him and celebrating his good health. After everything he had gone through, each second I could share with him now was like a gift to be treasured. It was the most trouble-free year of his life so far.

Five years old

At five years old, Christopher began attending a preschool program for handicapped children. It was a difficult transition for both of us, but it was the only way to prepare him for kindergarten. Due to his worsening scoliosis (abnormal curvature of the spine), he had also been followed for years by an orthopedic surgeon, who now felt it was time to fit Christopher for a back brace. He was expected to wear the brace for twenty-three hours each day and also attended physical therapy to increase his upper body strength. Though his lung capacity was quite limited, he tolerated the brace well, calling it his "suit of armor." On January 9, 1991, I gave birth to a healthy and beautiful baby girl, whom we named Chelsea. Christopher was proud to be a big brother, and life was feeling more normal and complete than ever.

By six years old, Christopher was diagnosed with attention deficit hyperactivity disorder (ADHD). He was classified as perceptually impaired and placed in a special education kindergarten program within our district. His separation anxiety worsened to the degree that he dreaded going to school, afraid that he would never see me again. He did not know how to adjust to the real world when all he knew was the medical world. It was the only place he felt safe. I learned everything I could about ADHD and learning disabilities, so that I could be an advocate for my son. I also trusted the child study team and special education teachers and followed their recommendations for placement. On September 9, 1992, our third child Nicholas was born, about six years after I first gave birth to Christopher. Nick was a healthy and easygoing baby. Our family felt complete.

At seven, Christopher was taking weekly karate lessons, playing on a basketball team, and riding his dirt bike motorcycle with his father. He loved being busy all the time. We made several changes to his medication throughout the year for his ADHD, hoping to improve his ability to focus. He also was anxious and impulsive, which made it particularly difficult for him to learn. Christopher still had medical issues to take of as well. At this time, he was using an inhaler for asthma, taking medication for recurrent GI reflux, and continuing to wear his brace. We both struggled, but strived to remain strong and intact.

School became the greatest challenge for Christopher. He feared going to school, and everybody had his or her own beliefs about why he felt this way, but whatever the reason, I knew his fear was real and justified. He was tired of getting sick, taking pills and sprays, wearing a brace, and feeling different than his peers. He also suffered migraine headaches and numerous bouts of pneumonia, and he slowly began to withdraw from all social events.

I wondered, as I am sure Christopher did, when it would all end. It was a difficult task juggling Christopher's medical needs with those of the rest of the family, and at the same time, somehow, maintaining a sense of peace and normalcy in our daily life. It was a large responsibility—a challenge that I faced head-on each day. Fortunately, while attending a local support group, I met a wonderful child psychologist who listened intently to my story and felt she could help Christopher ease his vulnerability. We met with her, and through months of intense counseling and play therapy, Christopher began to overcome many of his fears and insecurities. I learned to let go and let him be his own person.

Christopher remained in a special education class at our local public school for three years. In addition, he received tutoring and counseling at home. Despite our efforts, however, our child still feared school. The social phobias, separation anxiety, and fear of academic failure, crippled his ability to be happy or successful.

I went on a mission throughout New Jersey searching for a school that could meet his specific needs. Christopher had average to above average intelligence, specific learning disabilities, and ADHD. There were no limitations to his physical capabilities. Within six months, I believed I had found the perfect school for my son. However, it took an additional six months to convince my husband and local school district to send him to a private school. It was not that our community school did anything wrong or was deficient—it was that Christopher needed much more structure and one-on-one instruction.

As fourth grade rolled around, Christopher finally began attending The Newgrange School in Trenton, NJ. It was apparent from the first day that Christopher had found a new home; he would fit in here. His quality of life quickly improved as he adjusted to the new environment and made new friends. In time, Christopher even learned to take pride in his work and enjoy going to school.

Looking Back

Christopher had an extraordinary ability of overcoming not only physical distress, but also the emotional. After everything he had been through, it was a miracle he was able to live a normal life. I, on the other hand, suffered from post-traumatic stress disorder (PTSD). Constantly fearing his future and haunted by memories of his past, I was plagued with anxiety. I sought counseling for myself and began dealing with these issues. My friends and family did not understand; I was often told to leave the past behind me and to move forward, but a part of me did not want to forget. My counselor helped me to understand that even though Christopher's future was uncertain, my experience and knowledge were invaluable to others going through similar hardships. Thus, I began doing what I could to offer that experience back to the community. At an annual ECMO reunion in Boston, I created an ECMO parent support group. With Elaine's help, this led to a bi-monthly newsletter, quarterly meetings in Boston, and friendships with other ECMO families.

When Christopher turned ten years old, I started putting this story down on paper. Writing my recollections has been a tremendous process of growth and healing. These memories were painful to recall at times, but I endured because I felt strongly about preserving the experiences, so that I could embrace it and others could learn from it. I want parents to know they are not alone. It is exhausting yet rewarding to raise a medically-fragile baby. I felt it was my responsibility to accommodate my son and help him achieve the expectations his teachers, peers, and family would have on any normal child, while developing my own reasonable goals for Christopher without fostering self-pity or helplessness. I had to be willing to let him stumble and grow, and he did. Christopher grew to be a unique and independent person, able to live and work on his own.

I also wanted health professionals to be able to recognize the extent of their influence on a child and his family, even years down the road. Some of Christopher's nurses and doctors were absolute blessings, angels sent to watch over my baby. Others made me question humanity.

A good parent-professional relationship is based on mutual respect, trust, and honesty. I have been extremely fortunate to have so many compassionate and committed health professionals caring for Christopher, particularly in Boston Children's Hospital. The characteristics that set them apart were their willingness to truly listen and keep an open mind. A good pediatrician recognizes that parents know their children best. Furthermore, the doctors in Boston knew to observe each patient as a whole. Christopher was not a set of pieces to be scrutinized through the lens of one specific medical specialty. To the pulmonologists, he was not just a defective pair of lungs, and to the cardiologists, he was not a malfunctioning heart, but a complex human being with a diverse array of inseparable physical and emotional traits.

Looking back, I have determined that it is through human experience that we witness God's unending love. Christopher's survival was the result of years of intense medical research, determination, and commitment of caring and compassionate health professionals. Meanwhile, the preservation of his and my emotional wellness was owed to family, friends, and community. Their love and support gave us the strength to persevere in the darkest of times. I thank God for all the people who have positively impacted my life, and I pray for the ability to pay it forward.

*****

Our lives have much greater meaning than we may be able to appreciate in the moment. There were numerous times when I felt like giving up hope, but I chose to put my faith in God instead. Success comes in due time, not necessarily our time, and by trusting in God, I eventually saw good prevail. On good days, Christopher was on top of the world, but on bad days, he reminded me how difficult life could be and how hard he had to struggle. He would often say, "Mom, it would be easier to be an angel in heaven with God." I would hold back my tears and firmly assured him that God had a special plan for him. I also often reminded him, "You are my angel here on Earth."

A baby from Ewing fights to beat the odds

Infant suffers from rare condition

By MONITA CASEY
Staff Writer

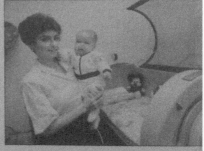

Suzanne Cavalier holds 7-month-old Christopher, her son, near the ventilator where he sleeps. He has had constant medical attention since birth.

▶ see MIRACLE, A18

Christopher Cavalier and his father are appreciative of the efforts made by the community to alleviate the high medical and travel costs of his illness.

Baby Christopher Fund
helps fighting 8-month old

By Alison McCuaig

How you can help

If you want to contribute to the Baby Christopher Fund, please mail your check to: Barbara and Fred Miller, Box 44, Neduland Avenue, Titusville, N.J. 08560.

Founding father of ECMO;
Robert Bartlett, M.D., University of Michigan

Surgeon Craig W. Lillehei, M.D. with his "star" patient

Oxygen free for the first time at age 3 with
Pulmonologist Marc B. Hershenson, M.D.

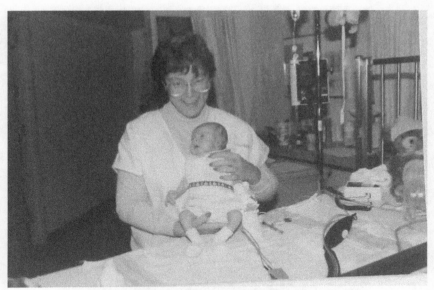

Smooth Sailed off ECMO.
Primary nurse Elaine Caron, R.N.

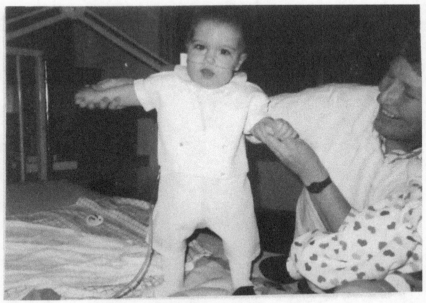

Christening outfit Debut;
with help from Margie Smith, R.N.

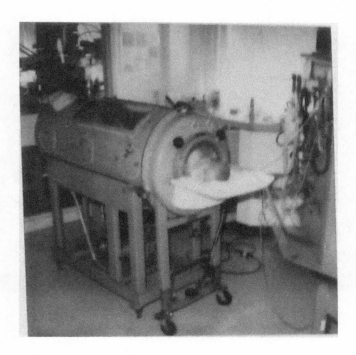

The iron lung!
Negative pressure ventilator

Summers at the beach are always best with family.

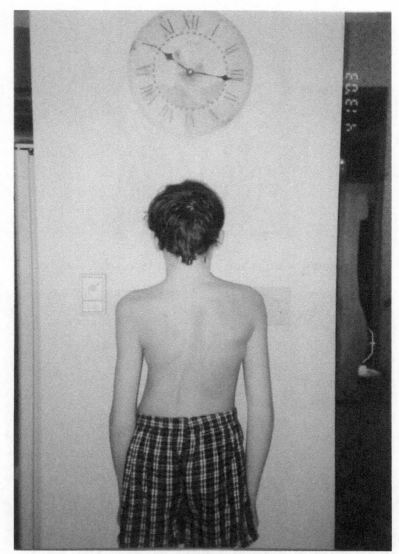

April 2003, two days before scoliosis repair.

Three month check up with Orthopedic
Surgeon, John Emans, M.D.

Christopher and ICU nurse Pat Berry, R.N.

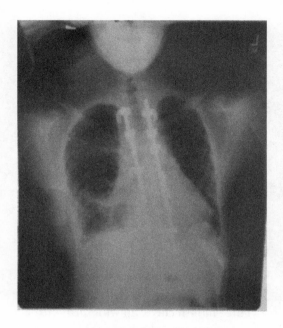

Anterior and Posterior Spinal Fusion

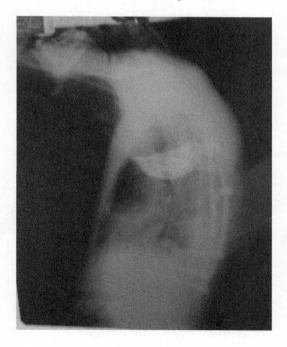

Chris and Dave, best friends since middle school at Newgrange

My three loves, Christopher, Chelsea, and Nicholas

Two best grandmothers in the world,
grandmom Elsie and Memam Madge

Happy 30th Birthday Christopher!

God, Why Am I Here?
Christopher Cavalier

Early Signs of Trouble

I was born in New Jersey with a congenital diaphragmatic hernia; there was a hole in my diaphragm that allowed my abdominal organs to migrate up to my heart and lungs. After the doctors cut me open and patched up my diaphragm, they realized I would not survive without mechanical assistance. My lungs and heart were unable to sufficiently oxygenate my blood, so I was sent to Boston Children's Hospital to be treated by extracorporeal membrane oxygenation (ECMO), which allowed my body to rest while the machine acted like an external set of artificial lungs.

I lived at home with an oxygen tank, and after some time, I was able to breathe on my own. The first three years of my life were spent on oxygen, tube feedings, and several visits to the hospital for heart failure. These were the most precarious years of my life, but they were far from the end of my struggles.

Back Problems

At the age of five I was told that I had scoliosis: an abnormal sideways curvature of the spine. Mine was severe. I did not feel any pain, but it did throw my back out of alignment, and my doctors made us aware of the potential problems that this could cause in the future. This would include problems such as difficulty in breathing, pain, lack of mobility, and disfigurement. They suggested that I get surgery to correct the problem, but at five years old, they felt I was still too young for the operation. Instead, I was given a brace to help straighten out my back. The plan was to give me some time to grow before having the surgery and possibly even avoid it completely.

The braces that I have worn through the years have been made of metal and hard plastic. They covered me from my underarms to my waist. Latches on the back could be unfastened to allow me to fit in the brace, and then they would be tightened once properly fitted. I always wore it under my shirt, so most people would have no idea

I had it on. As a kid, I liked to think of myself as the Terminator because of the metal that encased my upper body.

As my body grew, I continually had to be fitted for new braces. During a fitting, I would be taken to the back room of a doctor's office, while only wearing my underpants and a T-shirt. Eventually, the doctor would walk in, holding a bucket of warm water and a roll of plaster. He would then have me stand still with my arms raised as he dipped the plaster in the water and began wrapping it around my upper body. After I was covered from my waist to my armpits, the doctor would then push my back into the desired position and hold me there until the plaster hardened. This grew increasingly painful as I got older.

When everything had hardened and dried, I would be told to lie down on a bench face up, so the doctor could begin to cut me free. The doctor used a saw that was specially designed to cut off the plaster without going through my skin. Instead of the saw circling around, it quickly went back and forth. It was created this way so that if it happened to touch my skin, it wouldn't tear through. However, if force were applied, it would cut through my flesh like a knife through butter.

With my face covered, he would start at the top of my neck or groin and start sawing in the opposite direction. I can still remember feeling the saw as it made contact with my T-shirt. It kind of tickled and made me want to move around. Slowly, he would work his way through as I felt flecks of plaster flying off. When he was done, the doctor would put the saw down and pry the plaster open with his hands. I would sit up and rise out of the plaster that had now become a mold of my upper body.

The mold was used as a blueprint for the structure of my next brace. Once I was given the new braceI was required to wear it twenty-four hours a day. I went through this process multiple times in my youth.

Death

When I was younger, there was one thing that I feared above all else: death. It may seem like a silly thing to think about at a young age, but it was a big concern of mine. Though I was raised in a

Christian family, I never fully understood what happens after death, and it was terrifying to not know. I found the scariest part of death to be its inescapability. No matter how healthy you may be or how cautious you are, the day will come when you leave this earth.

One night, when I was around the age of seven, I was lying in my bed, thinking about what will happen when I die, and the idea was so scary that I got out of my bed, walked into the hall, and sat down on the floor crying. My dad found me there. He sat down and asked what was wrong, and I told him that I was afraid of dying. He held me and said that I had a long time to go before I died. I felt that knowledge slightly comforting, but the fear was still there.

Over the years, I went to church and gained a much better grasp of death. I learned that if you accept Jesus into your heart and believe that he died for your sins, you would go to heaven. While this abated some of my worries, it also created new ones. The scariest of these was the concept of hell. If there was anything I learned, hell is not the place that you want to end up. So I wasted no time in praying to God for forgiveness and inviting Jesus into my heart.

Over the course of my childhood and teen years I would continue to pray that same prayer in hopes that it would assure my entry into heaven. I saw heaven as privilege, and not as a guarantee. I felt that if I did something bad enough, I might be rejected from heaven.

My parents were aware of my fear and decided to buy me a book titled *Eternal Security*. The book answered a lot of my questions regarding the afterlife. It helped me understand that heaven is guaranteed to anyone who accepts Jesus into his or her life. I knew then that no matter what happens to me, heaven is waiting for me on the other side.

Yet, with all things taken into consideration, there was still a fear of dying. I've heard it said, "everyone wants to go to heaven, but no one wants to die". Well that's where I was at regarding my feelings about death. Even though I took comfort in going to heaven, the thought of dying still scared me. It was not until young adulthood that the fear of death would be eradicated from my mind.

School Problems

My problems with school truly began around first grade. Fitting into a classroom setting was difficult for me, simply because I learned better in a one-on-one setting. I had trouble keeping up with the lesson that was being taught because the teacher was addressing the whole class and going at their pace. I was too shy to ask questions, because I hated it when the entire class was staring at me. So while I would try to pay attention, my mind would inevitably wander off.

As hard as it was for me to get through the academic aspect of school, it was even harder for me to fit in with my classmates. I was very different from them, and they made sure that I knew it. They would call me various names and make fun of the way I looked. You could not have picked an easier target in the class. I was a skinny little kid who had to walk around wearing a brace made of metal and plaster underneath his shirt.

Soon, the bullying became more physical, especially once I hit second grade. Some kids would push me around while others would want to pick a fight. One of their favorite things to do was grab the handlebars on the back of my brace and swing me around. Surely I could have fought back, but I was always afraid that if I did, I would get into trouble, not to mention the fact that it was a group of kids against just me, so even if I did get a punch in, it would have just made them angry and increased my torment.

Recess was always the worst. During that time, I would just play on my own and keep an eye on the people around me. But somehow, a group of bullies would find the right opportunity to harass me. It soon got to the point where I would not go to recess at all. I would either spend my time eating lunch with one of the teachers or volunteer to help out in the school library. I did anything that I could to avoid going outside with the others.

Going to school was terrifying for me. I would go to extreme lengths to get out of class. On one occasion, I went into the school bathroom and hit my head against the wall in an effort to make myself sick so that I could go home. My parents had me set up with a psychiatrist to talk about my fears of going to school, along with other fears that I had as a kid, such as getting lost and being left alone.

I told the psychiatrist how I hated going to school and would do just about anything to get out of going. She came up with the idea of bribing me to face my fears. Each week I would have to go to school without giving my mom any trouble. If I cooperated, she would have a new toy waiting for me during my next visit. I can see how she was trying to help me, but in the end, it only taught me how to keep my mouth shut so I could collect my prize at the end.

As time passed, my hatred for school continued to grow. It got to the point where the slightest taunt or push triggered me to push back. I knew I could not get into a fistfight with them because of my size and limited movement, so I instead found that shoving them into a wall or onto the ground was enough to get them to leave me alone.

After the third grade, my mom decided that I had to be moved to a different school. As much as I hated where I was, I feared the idea of going to another school that I was not familiar with. What made things worse is that the school my mom found was located a half-hour away from my home. Even after making a visit to the school and meeting all the nice teachers and students, it still did not justify the transition for me, but Mom was convinced that this was the right thing to do. So after getting through third grade, I was sent to a school for children with learning disabilities.

On the first day of school, I was extremely nervous, but the teachers were kind enough to personally guide me around the building. I found my classroom and took a seat at my desk. I looked around at my classmates with great interest. Since the school was for anyone with a learning disability, kids came from all over New Jersey. Almost every student came from a different ethnic background.

After everyone had arrived, we were given time to talk with one another. Some took up the offer while others sat in their seat quietly. Eventually, everyone in the school was told to head down to the gym so that the faculty could tell us what the school had in store for us. While we sat in rows of bleachers, waiting for the presentation to start, I started talking with one of my classmates sitting next to me. I do not recall who started up the conversation, but I do remember that we hit it off very well. As the principal started to speak, he extended a hand towards me and said, "My name's Mike." I shook his hand and said, "I'm Chris." At that moment, I had not only made a best friend, but I also knew that I was in the right place.

As time passed, my number of friends continued to grow, and I soon considered the school to be like a second home for me. I even looked forward to going to school, since that was normally the only time my friends and I saw each other. The sense of belonging that I felt made it much easier for me to learn and improve my academic skills.

Even though I got out of the nightmare that was my old school, I carried with me a burning hatred for those who pick on others. Nothing gets under my skin like seeing or hearing about someone getting pushed around by other people. When I see in the media how a student has committed suicide due to bullying, I feel a great deal of sadness for them, as well as anger that a person could unnoticeably be pushed to the point of taking their own life.

One of the things that I cannot stand is when teachers show favoritism for some students over others. Now I am not talking about a teacher who takes a liking to a student and gives them some extra help or attention. I am referring to watching teachers treat some students better than others. I have seen the following situation unfold multiple times: Students will be picking on one of their classmates without a word of intervention from the teacher. Then when that student tries to defend himself, he or she ends up getting punished for it. It was always disturbing to me when I saw that happen.

Comments about School and Life

If you are reading this and dealing with problematic individuals in your school, I encourage you to hang in there. Whoever you were in school will not matter once you get into the world. School is only a small part of life, and once it is over, it is done. We have all heard of the "loser" who has gone on to lead a huge successful life, as well as the high school hotshot who is now struggling in the real world.

Most would probably say that this is because one spent more time getting smarter while the other refused to do school work, but I do not believe that it is intelligence that has lead these individuals down their paths. I feel it is their ability to get along with other people. Many people hold onto the concept of lumping others into groups. They are often disrespectful to those who they feel are below them, and this attitude will cause them to have multiple problems in their lives.

One issue this will raise is their lack of ability to cope with different people and the environments around them. When they were in school, all the students they knew most likely came from a similar background. They got used to being the tough one at their school and believe this attitude will work after graduation, but in the real world, people are not submissive and do not offer assistance to those who seem pretentious or rigid.

This will lead them to the biggest disadvantage in life: missing out on various opportunities. I attribute much of my success to meeting the right people and working with them to provide each other with support in whatever we needed help accomplishing. A person who is not accustomed to properly interacting with strangers will most likely miss out on meeting the person who could have made their life easier simply because they do not do well with others.

The people who know what it feels like to be put down tend to be much more accepting of others and their differences. This will lead them to meeting a person who has the potential to change their lives for the better. Treating others with kindness and respect is the key to making connections and receiving their support in turn. This is why, regardless of the profession you aim for, every college and employer wants you to learn how to effectively communicate with people.

I have heard of many employers, such as my father, say that it is hard to find good employees because most do not follow or understand the fundamentals of job expectations. He told me that the two most common reasons he had to let go of an employee were that person's inability to show up on time and their lack of respect for customers. Those two factors mattered more to him then that person's education or intelligence.

All for Nothing

Around my fifteenth birthday, my mom and I went to the doctor to get a checkup on the progress of my scoliosis. I entered the waiting room to find numerous patients who suffered from various orthopedic problems. I sat down in one of the chairs while my mom signed us in. As I looked around the room, I noticed all the people who wore braces like me. Each brace had been created to correct a different problem with their body. Though I felt sorry for them, I had grown accustomed to seeing people in such conditions.

One thing I never got used to, though, was looking in the play area and finding young children around ages four to eight playing with toys, completely oblivious to the fact that their bodies were encased in their own miniature braces. The sight made me sad to know the pain and discomfort that they would continue to go through over the course of their lives.

After about a half-hour of waiting, my mom and I were taken to our room. I was fitted into a patient gown and waited another half-hour for the doctor to arrive. When the doctor entered the room, he kindly greeted us and got to work. He gave us a series of questions concerning my back and then gave me a physical examination, checking to see if I could walk properly and how flexibly my body could move. When he was satisfied, he guided me into the X-ray room.

The room was cold. The pair of underwear and the gown that was given to me did little to protect me from that cold. A weight was tied around my waist, and I stood in front of the X-ray machine. I stood in different positions, and was asked to stay still and hold my breath whenever the technologist left the room to take an X-ray. When they were done, I was sent back to the room where my mom was waiting.

When I had finished putting my clothes back on, the doctor took us into his office. He took my new X-ray films out of a big envelope and placed them in a rectangular holder that gave off white light, allowing us to clearly see the image. What I saw was a picture of my spine noticeably curved from side to side in the shape of an S. The doctor explained that my curve had gotten increasingly worse, so bad that I would need to get the corrective surgery after all.

My heart sank upon hearing the bad news that he was giving me. Fear crept into my chest; I knew what type of surgery he was talking about. The surgery was called a spinal fusion. The idea of the surgery was to straighten the spine, then hold it in place by fusing some of the vertebrae together. Two titanium bars would also be screwed into the spine to maintain straightness. I had spent ten years of my life wearing a brace so that I could prevent myself from having the surgery, but all it did was buy me some time before the curve got too severe.

The doctor went on to explain the surgery, but I hardly paid much attention to what he was saying. I was lost in my thoughts, thinking about how this turn of events could happen so suddenly. I had only come in for a checkup, and was now being told that I was going to need major surgery. When the doctor was finished talking, we left his office and went to the front desk to sign out. Then we headed back to my mom's car in the parking lot.

When we got inside the car, the idea of surgery had become too much for me. I let go of all the emotion that was built up inside me and I began to cry. I was afraid that I might die during the surgery. Though death was normally a rare complication from this surgery, I had some other medical issues that went against my chances of survival. My mom did her best to comfort me and tell me that everything was going to be fine. Her words did little to soothe me, though. I knew the risks that I would face. The predicament preoccupied my thoughts for the whole ride home. I had one year to prepare myself for the surgery that was to come.

The Big Day

On the day of the surgery, I felt that I was ready for whatever might happen. We left our hotel. It was early morning, and I was not allowed to eat anything before the surgery. Slowly we made our way to Boston Children's Hospital. The city still seemed to be asleep. I marveled at the sky and the wind that blew by me. The warmth that I felt from the sun brought comfort to my body. I took notice of every aspect of life that was around me, because it might be my last chance to do so.

When we were inside the building, we went to the waiting room to wait for me to be called. The room was filled with parents and their children. Some of the people looked upset, while others cried. Some were calmer than others. I had expected myself to be scared for my life, but I hardly felt anything other than some anxiety. I felt this way because during the past year of preparation, my faith in God had grown tremendously. I was fully aware that I could die from the operation, but knew that if I did, I would go to heaven. That gave me peace in my heart—that no matter what the outcome was, everything was going to be okay.

I sat down in a chair with my family and asked my parents for the Simpsons comic book that they had purchased for me the previous night. After a period of time waiting, the doctor called us. My family and a couple of others got up and followed the doctor. He led us to a room where I would be prepped for surgery. The doctor sat me down on a bed as I waited for him. I managed to get a few more pages of my comic book in before the doctor returned with a needle in hand. After he cleaned my arm with a sterilizer, he pushed the needle into my vein and connected it up to a tube that injected a liquid into my arm. The doctor waited a while longer to let the medicine take effect. When he felt that I was ready, he wheeled me toward the doors of the operating room.

Entering a World of Pain

Before I went through the doors, I noticed my mom's eyes began to tear up. "Don't worry Mom," I told her. "This is going to be a walk in the park." That is the last thing I can remember before I went into the operating room. My mom claims that I was awake on the operating table before they got started, but I have no recollection of it. I do not have a good memory of what happened during my first days of recovery either, so I will do the best that I can. However, the next thing I remember is waking up, lying in a recovery bed with my mom sitting next to me. When I was aware of what was going on, I looked up at the sky and said, "Thank you, God."

Then before I could do anything else, I was hit with an explosion of pain. It was beyond anything I had ever felt before. I don't have a good way to describe what it felt like, but it was like being burned, stretched, and twisted from the inside out. Every action I made, even breathing, gave off another wave of torment that spread throughout my body. Then I realized how hungry and thirsty I was. I asked for something to drink, but the doctor could not give me anything because my stomach was not completely functioning yet. I started crying because of the torture I was feeling, which only made things worse. With every sob, a wave of pain coursed through my body, each one worse than the last. I do not know how many days I suffered like that, but they were horrible.

I would lie in the bed, wishing that the pain would end and being certain that I was dying. I begged God to make the pain go away any way he could. I even asked my mom through tear-streaked eyes to let me die and end the pain. She would hold me close to her and tell me that everything was going to be okay in the end, but I did not want to wait that long. I wanted this to be over. So I lay there and dealt with my situation as best I could. At the time, I wished that I had just died on the operating table.

There is little else that I remember during the first few days, but I do remember when I got my first "meal." It was late at night, and a nurse was watching over me. Night was my least favorite time of the day, because I would have to yawn, and when I tried to yawn, pain would build in my chest that was so unbearable I would have to cut myself off before I could fully inhale. I was partially awake with my parents next to me in a chair. The nurse came over and offered me one of the small plastic cups that they use to hold pills. The cup was filled about three-fourths of the way up with chipped ice. The nurse told me I could eat the ice, but I could only get one cup about every hour. With effort I took the cup from her hand and dumped the ice into my mouth. It was the greatest thing I had ever tasted in my life. As the ice melted, it quenched a bit of my thirst and helped to wet my overly dry mouth.

When I finished the ice, I asked for another cup, but she insisted that I had to wait another hour. Reluctantly, I waited in my bed and watched the clock. I tried to get some sleep, but it was hopeless. I was in pain and discomfort that kept me from getting a good night's rest. Eventually, the hour passed, and I was handed my second serving. I plopped the ice onto my tongue and let it melt into water. When finished, I handed the cup back to the nurse and waited another hour.

After resting and recovering for a while, the doctors felt that I was ready to begin physical therapy. During my first therapy session, a woman who walked into the room helped me turn onto my left side (because my right side still had stitches), and began repeatedly hitting me in the back with her fists. The idea was to help get the mucous out of my lungs by moving it around. The punches were not too hard; they were about the same force as someone who would playfully hit a friend. To most people, it would hardly even feel painful. It might even feel like an aggressive back massage, but for me, it felt like I was being hit with a hammer.

For a brief time, I ignored the excruciating agony that was going through my body. However, the pain quickly began to build on itself, and it became too much for me to handle. I begged her to stop what she was doing, but she insisted that this needed to be done. My mom held me in place so that I could not roll onto my back. She had tears in her eyes as she watched me suffer. When it became too much for her, she stopped, and another woman took her place. In my frustration I cried while the exercise continued. When it was finally over, I was rolled onto my back and was allowed to relax.

When the doctor decided that I was well enough, I was moved from the emergency room to the recovery room. I shared my new room with another boy, and I liked the fact that I was able to watch TV from my bed. The room was also more luxurious with a desk next to the bed and chairs for my family. The only thing missing was a video game system. From my previous hospital experiences, I recalled they could roll a TV into the room that was hooked up to a system. So I asked the nurse if she could bring any video games into my room, but she told me that if I wanted to play video games, I would have to walk to one of the game rooms down the hall. My heart sank upon hearing the bad news. I could barely roll over in my bed, let alone walk down a hallway. So I just lay in my bed and watched what was on TV.

I stayed in my bed for a couple more days. My only physical activity was clicking the remote to change a channel and receiving more therapy on my back. Each time the nurse came back, the treatment got slightly better, and I was almost able to tolerate the exercise, but the pain never fully went away.

Finally, the day came that I would try to walk again. A nurse came into the room with a wheelchair and said that today I was going to walk. The nurse told me that there was a specific way to sit up from the bed that she would like me to try. First, I was turned to my left side so that I was on my shoulder and facing the wall. Then I let my legs go down from the side as the upper half of my body was turned up right so that I was in a sitting position. My mom and a nurse helped me get off of the bed and into a wheelchair.

They wheeled me into a hall to see how I would do out of the room. Then my mom and the nurse lifted me out of the chair. I did my best to help out, but it was not easy for me to support my own weight. When I was ready, I tried taking my first step while they held my arms. I lifted my leg and was about to put it in front of me when the full weight of my body wound up on my back leg, and I began to fall forward. I put my other leg out in front to catch myself, but my foot landed at a bad angle, and I began to stumble. My mom and the nurse held onto me and kept me from falling.

The rest of the steps that I took ended in the same fashion. This exercise went on until my body was too tired to continue. When it was over, I was put back in my wheelchair and pushed back to my room. Once inside the room, they helped me up from the chair and onto the mattress. From there I laid back down the same way that I got up. I fell onto my left shoulder, rolled onto my back, and was able to relax in my bed.

Getting Back On My Feet

As the days went by, I got better at walking. My legs had gotten strong enough to support my body, and I had become more balanced, but I had to build up my stamina. I could only walk for a short while before my body became too tired to continue. The doctors decided I should get accustomed to walking on stairs. The nurse helped me walk to the physical therapy room with my mom at my side. I soon made it to the room where we would be doing the exercise.

The nurse presented me with wooden stairs that were used for the physical therapy training. She wanted me to walk up and down the stairs for exercise as many times as possible. It almost seemed like a joke, since there were only three or four steps and I had gotten my legs stronger by walking. I felt that this challenge should not be too much trouble. While the nurse held my hand, I put one foot onto the first step. The action put some slight strain on my leg, but it was not too bad. Then I had to get my other foot onto the first step. I started to lift my leg from the floor, but as soon as my toes left the ground, gravity seemed to greatly increase. I had fallen backwards, but the nurse held my arm and helped me land on my foot again. I decided to give it another try and braced myself for the weight. Putting all of my weight onto my front foot, I took a step up the stairs. It felt like I was wearing a backpack half-filled with rocks. My leg struggled with the weight, but I managed the climb. Once I was on the first step, I took a quick breather. It seemed funny that I had only stepped about six inches off of the ground and I was almost completely worn out. When I felt that I was ready, I continued up the stairs.

Once the therapy was over, I felt like I was going to pass out. My legs ached from all the stress that they had gone through, and my heart raced in my chest. I was out of breath, quickly breathing to fill my lungs with air. I tried to keep my breaths as shallow as possible, because if I breathed too deeply, that tremendous pain would build in my chest and cause me to cut my breath short. I was taken back to my room to rest.

After a week and a half, the doctor came to my room to see how my recovery was coming along. He checked to see how my scars had healed, and to see if I had enough strength to leave the hospital. The doctor gave me a few small tests to see how physically mobile I was. He wanted to see if I could get in and out of bed on my own, and if I could walk without much help. When finished, he said I could leave in the next day or two. Before he left, we took some photos together, and I thanked him for his excellent work.

Going Home

I was extremely happy when the day came for me to leave. When all my things were packed, I got into a wheelchair and was pushed to the hospital exit. From there, I had to walk to our hotel across the street. I was ready to collapse when we got to the room, especially since I had to walk up a flight of stairs, but everything was okay, and I had a good first night out of the hospital.

The next morning, we made our long drive back home. Though there was slight discomfort, I managed to get home without a problem. I was eager to be back in my own house and was ready to regain some of my daily life. However, I had to take it easy and spent most of my time in the living room playing video games, which is one of the best painkillers around. Breathing was my greatest difficulty while living at home. I had trouble filling my lungs with air, because each deep breath built pain in my chest. That meant that I could not yawn or laugh without feeling like my chest was burning.

I was given a breathing treatment machine that helped me take full deep breaths. The guy who had shipped the device came to our house to show me how to use it. It consisted of a small box and a plastic tube. He turned the machine on and told me to take a breath in from the tube. When I started to breathe in, I felt air being shot into my lungs. I panicked as my lungs were being pushed to capacity. I could feel the burning in my chest again, and I thought my lungs were going to burst. However, just when I thought I could not take any more air, the machine stopped. After the treatment, I was relieved, and I found myself able to breathe more freely. I had everything I needed to live comfortably at home.

After a year, I made a full recovery with minimal problems. At one point, I had gotten the brilliant idea of trying to climb on monkey bars. As soon as my feet left the ground, I felt like my arms had been ripped from their sockets, so I quickly dropped to the ground and decided to not try that again any time soon. Things were working out great for me when the recovery was over. I had gotten back in school and was happy to be with my friends. My family was back in their usual routine. I had gotten my license and even my first car. It seemed like things were going to be okay.

The Fun Isn't Over Yet

As my senior year of high school approached I was made aware of a problem developing inside me: hepatitis C. Hepatitis C is a viral infection of the liver that may not show any symptoms for years, but can cause severe liver problems down the road. What is really interesting is how I contracted the disease. Around the time of my birth, blood donors were not screened for hepatitis C. I underwent surgery and other procedures, and frequently required IV blood. Now about seventeen years later, I discover that one of my donors must have carried the virus. I was injected with contaminated blood. Can you believe that? Ever since that time the hepatitis had been growing inside me.

The treatment for getting rid of the hepatitis was not going to be simple either. Today, it can be treated relatively easily with pills, but back then, I was told I would have to inject medication into my thigh once every week until the hepatitis got destroyed. The length of time the treatment took depended on the patient's blood type. If the person had blood types B or C, the treatment would have to take a full year, whereas if you were lucky enough to have type A, it would only take six months. I can remember thinking to myself, *Can I please get a break on this one God?* I hoped and believed that I was type A; I wanted this to go by as quick as possible.

Alas, a simple blood test determined that I was not type A. As disheartening as this news was, I decided to go along with the treatment plan anyway. I wanted to get this over with now, instead of waiting until later in life. My mom and I were scheduled to come in one day to learn how to perform the treatment and get the supplies. Upon entering the room for the lesson, we noticed two syringes, a couple vials of liquid, and a box for trash.

The nurse made some final comments about how the medication would affect me, and then began to ask me some questions. I do not recall many questions, but one that sticks out in my mind is when she asked who would be performing the treatment. My mom and I had talked about this. Every time I imagined her performing the injection, I could see her hand shaking as the needle ripped through my skin. So I had decided that I would do it myself. With that out of the way, the nurse gave me a quick overview of how to perform the treatment.

First, I would need to mix the medication using a syringe, making sure to keep air out of the bottle. The nurse told me that every time that I use the needle to break through the top of the bottle, I should use a pad of rubbing alcohol to sterilize the surface. Then I would shake the bottle to make sure the meds blended together. While waiting for the bubbles in the bottle to subside, I would have to prepare for the injection. I had been told that the medication needed be injected into a part of my body that contained a good amount of fat. Since I was skinny, it was hard to find a good spot. Ultimately we decided my thigh was the best location.

When the nurse was done explaining the treatment, it was my turn to apply what I had learned. I opened the syringe packet and used it to mix together the meds. When I was done, I gently shook the bottle to blend the medication. Then I started to prepare my thigh for the injection. I used a pad of rubbing alcohol to clean the spot that the needle would enter. Then I opened the other syringe so I could use a needle that was cleaner. With the syringe in hand, I absorbed the proper amount of medication from the bottle and was ready for the injection.

I had a slight fear of needles. It always made me nervous when the doctors had to give me a shot. The sharp pain of medication being injected into my body was something I never looked forward to, but when I had to perform the injection myself, things went to a whole different level.

I took the needle and brought it to the spot where I would inject the medication, but I could not bring myself to pierce it through my skin. I could not physically move my hand. It was like my arm froze right before I could stick the needle through, keeping my body from harming itself.

My mom and the nurse asked me what was wrong. I told them that I was working up to it. I had absolutely no intention of backing out in front of the two of them. My mom told me to just quickly jab it in. I thought to myself, "Oh yeah, I'd like to see you try stabbing yourself with a needle." Regardless, I gave that method a try and it ended the same way, with my hand stopping in front of my leg.

For my last attempt, I tried to not think about what I was doing and pushed through my mental restraint. Slowly the needle broke through the skin and slid through my muscle. Then I started to inject the medication into my leg. My muscles started to burn from the medication, stretching them apart. Slowly but surely I emptied the syringe. I found it fascinating that I did not start to bleed when I took the needle out of my skin, and I was told it was because I was not injecting into a vein.

When I was done, we threw away the trash and packed up our things. The nurse gave us some final thoughts and we said goodbye. Now I would have to wait and see what side effects would occur from the drug. Things where fine for the ride home, but once we got into the house, the effects started. I had the symptoms of the flu attacking my body. I had a headache, nausea, and was overcome with chills. The effects lasted throughout the day.

Luckily, the next day I felt better. It was overwhelming that this could be the start of a yearlong process, but there was no backing down at this point. So when the next Thursday came, I was a bit concerned about what might happen. I went through the procedure and gave myself the shot. The side effects did take place again, however they were not nearly as bad as they had been before. Within a week or two more, there were no side effects at all.

The year passed with minor problems, other than my first car accident. I even became president of my school. For graduation, I gave a speech, thanking my friends, family, and the school, for all they had done for me. The injections were also going well. I would give myself a shot each Thursday after school and continue going about my day.

As the year started coming to its end, I had certain difficulties with the injection. First off, the smell of the alcohol wipes had become disturbing to me, probably because the smell made me think of what came next. Even today, the aroma reminds me of the injections. Another problem was that the skin on my leg had become scarred and tough. Just piercing the surface was like sticking a plastic needle through cardboard. I tried to perform the injection somewhere warm, because the cold made my skin and muscle tighter.

Once the needle was through, I would have to slowly inject the medication. If I did not give the medication enough time to sink in, a small bubble would start to form on my leg. I also found that my nerves had become more sensitive to pain. At times, it was almost like being injected with fire. In some cases, the pain would be too much, and I would try to find a spot with more tender flesh. This made the process more frustrating and annoying.

When I finally came to the end of my yearlong process, I was more than ready to end the shots. All I needed was a blood test to confirm that I was clean and I could be done. After receiving the results, however, it was still unclear whether I was free of the disease. It came into question if I should just stop the shots and take my chances, but if it turned out that I was still infected, then I would have to start the treatment over again. To be on the safe side, I decided to continue with the treatment.

After another few months, we ran into problems with the insurance company covering the treatment. While trying to get help, I started missing weeks without taking my shot. It was decided that too much time had passed to continue my treatment, so we went for one final blood test instead to see if I was still infected. The test came back negative, showing that I was free of hepatitis C.

Views

My Family

Throughout all of my medical trials, my family has been my support structure. My parents and I have always had a close relationship with one another. Mom and Dad made it a point to have family trips when we could all hang out and have a good time. From skiing to camping and going to the beach, these trips have given me many wonderful memories of the good times we have had.

Growing up, my mom was a stay-at-home mom. She made it her primary role in life to take care of my siblings and me. Mom would ensure that we had everything we needed for our daily activities. She drove us to school when we needed it, provided good food to eat, and made sure that we had whatever we needed at the house. If any of us had a problem, she was the first one to fight to protect us. Mom always wanted us to know that we had a loving, accepting home to which we could return.

My dad worked hard to provide for us. He put a tremendous number of hours into his business to make sure that he could give us what we needed. While he was committed to work, he also did his best to make time for us and took us on various trips together to bond and have fun. I especially loved going dirt biking together, whether in our backyard or at one of our secret spots. Dad always showed us how far he would go to guarantee that our family was provided for, happy, and safe.

My parents always made sure to let me know that they cared about me, and that they were there if I ever needed them. They helped me to endure my struggles, and gave me the strength and faith to get through everything. I cannot thank them enough for all the sacrifices that they made for me. I am sure it was difficult having me as a son. I thank them for hanging in there and sticking with each other.

If I had a list of people who I cared about and would go to the end of the earth to help, at the top would be my younger sister and brother. My sister Chelsea and I have gone to war with one another more times than I can count. As I'm writing this, I can remember watching one of our old VHS tapes of one of our earliest winters together, and there I was, throwing snowballs at my sister's head. Even if we sometimes fought, we still cared about each other greatly and had fun together.

One thing I know about my sister is she is a loving person and cares deeply for her family. Chelsea would not think twice about getting into a conflict with someone to protect us. Likewise, I would protect and help her if she ever had a problem. I know I was not always the best big brother and I am truly sorry for that, but I want her to know I love her and will always be there if she needs me.

My brother Nick and I have always been close. As kids, we have always played and stuck together. We would plan out various adventures and go exploring. He and I have done some pretty crazy and stupid things together. This included playing games like dirt bike soccer, which was when we would try and kick a soccer ball around the yard while riding our dirt bikes. We have had many great times together that I will always remember.

A buddy and I were laughing about how it is always the younger brother who is the cool one. Nick was always the adventurer in the family, trying out various sports and hobbies. I would also say that he is the smartest person in the family. I am proud of him for all of his accomplishments. All my friends know that I care deeply for my brother and will always have his back.

My sister and brother are the two most important people in the world to me. They have played a vital role in my life, and I have had many happy times with them. While we may live in different places and have different lives, I will always be looking out for them. I want them to know that I am always available to contact. If they were ever in trouble and needed me, I would be there so fast that by the time they got off the phone with me, I would already be standing behind them.

Life

When I was younger, I used to think life would be predictable. I would follow the course of getting a simple job, get married, have kids, retire, and die. It has not been even remotely that simple. All the plans I had for my life have been thrown out the window. Things are complex today with many problems and few viable solutions. It is so easy to become overwhelmed. I just do my best to adapt to situations and trust in God to see me through them.

One of the ways I cope with life is to disconnect from reality when things get to be too overwhelming, which is pretty much extreme daydreaming or even meditating if the term applies. I just imagine myself in some other place or far away. I also find that music is a good distraction from reality as well. However, I never overdo it. I know I do eventually have to come back to reality and deal with the problem.

I have met many people who have pretty much given up on life. I have lost count of the amount of people I know of who have thought of, attempted, or succeeded in committing suicide. I do not even get fazed anymore when people tell me they want to kill themselves. Instead of going into panic mode, which I have witnessed many people do when someone makes a statement like that, I just look at them—sometimes with a slight smile to let them know that I am not going to freak out on them—and I ask, "Okay, and why is that?"

When I respond in such a calm manner, they usually proceed to tell me what is going on. I could give specific stories about people whom I have spoken with about their suicidal thoughts, but I am not going to do that. These people shared very personal experiences with me, and I would be betraying their trust if I were to include them in this story. I will say that in my experience with people, the three most common things that drive people to suicide are the loss of a loved one, financial hardship, and stagnation in life.

I have found that not seeing progress in one's life or feeling like you are stuck or going backwards is the number one motivation for someone to commit suicide. All other forms of suffering may be manageable as long as you see that there is a way out. It is when you no longer see the light at the end of the tunnel that suicide starts to look like a viable solution to your problem.

I took the time to write this story to give others a message of hope and to let them know that even when it feels like your life is meaningless or has come to an end, there is no reason to give up. You have to take the problems you were given and find some way to overcome them. If you cannot overcome your problems, just push through them until they are over. Look for motivation in whatever form you can, even if that motivation sounds insane. Problems do eventually end, and even if they do not, there is always a way to manage them.

There is a positive side to taking on problems in life. The positive side is that each problem makes you a much more capable and resourceful person. Each challenge requires you to learn a new set of skills, and you develop a new awareness of people and life. Once you have finally made it through your personal tribulation, you will be able to leave the destruction behind and keep the gifts it has given you for the rest of your life.

Even with all the things I have had to deal with, people know me as a happy and fun individual. Friends say that I am a good person who cares about other people. Past employees have told me that they love having me as a manager, because I do not lose my temper on the job, and I try to be fair to everyone. Business owners that I have worked for have considered me to be one of their hardest workers and most-trusted employees or managers. They often trust me enough to give me the keys to their business and operate it while they are away.

I also manage to always find humor in life. Even in my worst situations, I can somehow find something funny that makes me laugh. Oftentimes I am laughing because a situation reminds me of something I saw in a movie or TV show. Though sometimes this irritates people because I probably should not be laughing in certain situations, such as when too many customers are ordering and the employees or managers start to have mental breakdowns. That is when I get yelled at, "Shut up, Chris! This isn't funny. We are in serious trouble right now. Stop laughing." At least, that is the PG version of what is usually said. However, I will always have at least one other person cracking up with me. I make it a point to be known by others as a happy person. I am happy, because no matter what others try to do to me, I have already won.

I was with a friend, and we were talking about life and our struggles. I said, "You know what the best part is about knowing God and that there is an afterlife? It is that this life is not the end. If I never get the life that I want, become the big success my family would like to see me become, get the family I want or the career I want, if my whole world comes crashing down, I have everything taken, and everyone is against me, it won't matter. With all of the uncertainties of life, the one thing guaranteed is that we are going to die, and I know that there is another life waiting for me after death." He agreed.

People

My view on people has changed considerably as I have grown older. I have found that people are like waves on the sea: they are unpredictable. There is really no way to know if someone is acting in your best interest or not. I have also learned that even if someone does believe they are acting in your best interest, they can still wind up hurting you and not even realize it.

It seems at times that I am just a living magnet for all the craziness of this world. Over my life, I have become aware of the harm that people are willing to do to one another, and it is shocking to me. Between my experiences with people and what I have heard from others, I have learned it is better to be cautious with others than to leave yourself in a vulnerable position. That does not mean that I do not like people, in fact I get along with most of the people that I meet. I just do not leave my personal wellbeing in their hands.

At this point, I do not believe in people; I only believe in God. Only God can know what is in my best interest and what moves I should make. Not believing in God and only believing that other people alone will do the right thing or make the right choice is a big mistake. When people are let down by others and do not have God to look to for guidance, they are more susceptible to give up on life. It is disturbing to me when someone I care about does not believe in God. I worry about what they will do when they get caught up in a bad situation and either will not or cannot go to anyone for help.

Furthermore, I am very cautious now with people who do not believe in God. It is not because I am afraid of them or do not like them—I just keep an eye out for them. I do that because a person who does not believe in God or believes that there is no ultimate consequence for their actions is capable of just about anything, so long as they believe they can get away with it.

With that being said, I have known some very good people in my life. All too often, these people have been through their own share of suffering, yet you would not know it because they hide it from others. This is why I make it a point to try and be nice to everyone. I do my best to never judge someone the first time I meet them. Since I am open with people about my weaknesses, they are open with me. This has given me the privilege to know and be friends with many great individuals.

Lastly, one of my greatest frustrations is not knowing whether or not friends from my past and present ever came to know God. I wonder if I could have done things differently or if I should have pushed harder. I hope that maybe someone else will help them or something will happen in their life that will help them see that God is real and that he loves them.

To my old friends who are no longer in my life, I want to thank you for all of the good times we had and for helping me when I needed it. Thank you for giving me the motivation to keep living when I had given up on this world. You were the best friends I could have asked for. I think about you often and pray that you are safe and doing well. I just wish that there was more I could have done to help you.

If I never shared my belief in Jesus Christ with you, I want you to know I am truly sorry. Just pray, ask for forgiveness for your sins, and ask Jesus to come into your heart to save you, and you will be saved. I would recommend getting a good Bible and start reading. Build your faith and relationship with Jesus. When I eventually pass away and get to heaven, I better find you there.

Who I Am

Not too long ago, I went through something of an identity crisis. I read somewhere that life is all about finding your identity or which people you identify with. So for fun I tried to figure out my identity or what group of people I would throw myself in with. I thought to myself about all the different hats I have had to wear throughout my life. I recalled the different positions that I have held, the friends I have had, and the different skills that I have developed.

I have found that I do not identify with any single group. In various situations, I have had to become different people in order to adapt. My experiences are so widespread that no one could ever fully understand me. Given that, I realized that who I am is dependent upon my relationship to the other person.

As for where I am and what I do today, it would be pointless to explain. By the time you read this, I may be in a different field and industry entirely. That is not entirely my choice; it is just the way the world works today. I am not trying to discuss economics, but holding multiple jobs and moving on to new ones seems to be a requirement for survival.

At some point, I may have a fixed career or one thing that I am known for, but I just do not see it. Things are changing faster than the average business can keep up with, and so they either change with it or go out of business. People have to be open to all opportunities out there or risk missing out on them. As for me, all I can do is keep adapting to the world the best I can and look to God for guidance, becoming whoever I need to become in order to make it in life.

Conclusion

After all the challenges I have gone through, I can honestly say that I am no longer afraid of death. That is not to say that when my time comes, I will not be scared, but I am no longer haunted by the idea of dying, especially since some of the medical procedures I endured felt worse to me than what death had to offer. It is my hope and prayer that when the time finally does come for me to pass away, I will be able to face it without fear.

A lot of people have asked how I can have such a strong faith in God. My answer would have to be that if there were no God, I would have died a long time ago. That also goes for anyone else who faced seemingly impossible odds. During my life, I have been cut open, operated on multiple times, had titanium fused to my bones, been burned, poisoned, drowned, suffocated, been pushed over the edge mentally multiple times, and forced to endure more pain than I could have ever handled, yet for reasons I may never fully understand, I am still here.

About the Author

Suzanne is a wife and mother of three children: Nicholas, Chelsea, and Christopher Cavalier. She was just twenty-two years old when she gave birth to her firstborn, Christopher. Entirely unprepared for the difficulties of raising an ill child thirty years ago, she and her husband Christopher began their relentless pursuit of faith, hope, and love. Her children now live on their own, and Suzanne resides with her husband in New Jersey. Having successfully raised her own family, she now drives a school bus in the interest of continued engagement with children. She spends her summers at the beach.

Christopher currently lives and works on his own in Monmouth County, New Jersey. He graduated from Monmouth University with a bachelor's degree in communications, and he loves to work. Christopher embraces his past and continues to endure the trials of adult life. He began writing and speaking about his experiences at age twenty to encourage others. He has a website to help share his story and message of hope: ecmosurvivor.com.

> 1 Corinthians 15:10 KJV: But by the grace of God I am what I am: and his grace which was bestowed upon me was not in vain; but I labored more abundantly than they all: yet not I, but the grace of God which was with me.